HIGH-PERFORMANCE
SOCCER

PAUL CALIGIURI
with Dan Herbst

HUMAN KINETICS

Library of Congress Cataloging-in-Publication Data

Caligiuri, Paul
   High-performance soccer / Paul Caligiuri with Dan Herbst.
     p. cm.
   Includes index.
   ISBN 0-88011-552-1
   1. Soccer--Training. I. Herbst, Dan. II. Title.
   GV943.9.T7C35   1997
   796.334'07--dc20   96-15783
                                       CIP

ISBN: 0-88011-552-1

Acquisitions Editor: Ken Mange; **Developmental Editor:** Marni Basic; **Assistant Editors:** Susan Moore-Kruse, John Wentworth, and Jacqueline Eaton Blakley; **Editorial Assistant:** Amy Carnes; **Copyeditor:** John Wentworth; **Proofreader:** Robert Replinger; **Graphic Designer:** Robert Reuther; **Graphic Artist:** Julie Overholt; **Photo Editor:** Boyd LaFoon; **Cover Designer:** Jack Davis; **Photographer (cover):** Wilfried Witters/Hamburg; **Photographers (interior):** Dan Herbst, Steve Slade, Jon Van Woerden, and Wilfried Witters/Hamburg; **Illustrator:** Jennifer Delmotte; **Printer:** United Graphics

Human Kinetics books are available at special discounts for bulk purchase. Special editions or book excerpts can also be created to specification. For details, contact the Special Sales Manager at Human Kinetics.

Printed in the United States of America   10 9 8 7 6 5 4 3 2 1

Human Kinetics
Web site: http://www.humankinetics.com/

United States: Human Kinetics, P.O. Box 5076, Champaign, IL 61825-5076
1-800-747-4457
e-mail: humank@hkusa.com

Canada: Human Kinetics, Box 24040, Windsor, ON N8Y 4Y9
1-800-465-7301 (in Canada only)
e-mail: humank@hkcanada.com

Europe: Human Kinetics, P.O. Box IW14, Leeds LS16 6TR, United Kingdom
(44) 1132 781708
e-mail: humank@hkeurope.com

Australia: Human Kinetics, 57A Price Avenue, Lower Mitcham, South Australia 5062
(08) 277 1555
e-mail: humank@hkaustralia.com

New Zealand: Human Kinetics, P.O. Box 105-231, Auckland 1
(09) 523 3462
e-mail: humank@hknewz.com

Contents

· ·

Foreword

In 1994, I represented my country in the World Cup. After that, I played one season with England's Coventry City before signing in Brazil. I'm now playing for the Los Angeles Galaxy. I'm not so sure that I could make those statements today if not for Paul Caligiuri.

It was Paul who, along with Peter Vermes, opened doors that were previously closed to American soccer players by first proving that we could successfully play top-level league football abroad. He accomplished that after leading our alma mater, UCLA, to its first NCAA Division I soccer national championship in 1985 in an 1-0 eight-overtime conquest of American University, in which Paul was named the title game's defensive MVP.

It was Paul who distinguished himself as the lone American representative in the 1986 FIFA World All-Star Game when he helped to set up Diego Maradona's late-game equalizer in front of a huge Rose Bowl crowd and a global television audience. That honor is one of many, including having played in the 1988 Summer Olympic Games; being one of only two American field players to start all seven U.S. games in both the 1990 and 1994 World Cups; leading the USA to two U.S. Cup championships, to the 1991 CONCACAF Gold Cup crown, and to a fourth-place finish in the 1995 Copa America (in which he became the 26th player in the history of the sport to earn his 100th cap when his work as a sweeper led us to our remarkable 3-0 upset of mighty Argentina).

But, mostly, it was Paul whose incredible 30-yard volley against Trinidad and Tobago in 1989 earned the USA our first World Cup berth in 40 years (which I'm convinced was the moment when American soccer finally came of age). Quite fittingly, it was Paul who then scored our first goal in that World Cup with a great solo dash against the Czechs.

And now it's Paul who has gathered together his years of experience to produce a book that he hopes will help one of you who is reading this to take America to the next level in which we seriously contend for the World Cup.

Paul and I are products of the American youth soccer system. We were once where you are now. That's why Paul's perspectives are so valid and valuable. On the pages ahead you'll learn what initiatives he undertook to get where he is today. I can vouch that his tales of his passion for the game and an unbridled desire to play it whenever possible are a common thread that runs throughout our National Team's roster.

Paul will offer scores of activities that you can do on your own or with a few friends to improve your skills. He will speak to the mindset that's required for you to fulfill your potential. And he'll provide insights into what steps you should take to increase your chances of not only playing college soccer but receiving financial aid to do so.

I know that I have greatly benefitted from Paul's guidance over the years. And I'm happy to say that the same high-quality advice is now available for you. My only regret is that this book wasn't written when I was 16!

Cobi Jones

Cobi in action for the U.S. National Team.

Preface

Fulfilling your potential in any endeavor doesn't happen by accident. That you're about to tackle these pages tells me you're a motivated athlete who wants to learn how to become the best soccer player you can be. Why did you pick up this book? I think it's because you're ready to take the next step and commit to making soccer an integral part of your life. You're ready to get serious—ready for information on how to achieve soccer success. You picked up the right book.

In a lifetime of playing soccer, I've discovered that the margin between those who reach the highest levels of the game and those with great talent who fall by the wayside is often very slim. If you're determined to work hard, I'll give you the tips you need to make sure your time is well spent and purposeful. This formula will take you beyond those whose genetic advantages aren't matched by a requisite amount of determination and knowledge.

That's why I wrote this book—to give you, the serious player, a tool to use as you take the steps to becoming as good as your potential will permit. You'll learn what my U.S. National teammates and I did during our developmental years to get where we are today.

I consider myself fortunate to have enjoyed a career in which I've been able to live out my wildest dreams. Much of my success I owe to the many outstanding coaches who helped me develop. But a large part of the equation was the thousands of hours I spent working on my own and my willingness to endure and overcome hardships.

If you're lucky enough to play for a top-caliber team with a first-rate coach, you've got a great headstart on most of your peers. But such a start will only give you an edge on the competition if you're sufficiently driven to put in those vital extra hours of work. These hours can be boring, yes, and lonely, but above all they can be extraordinarily productive. In the long-term you'll find they were the smartest and best hours you ever spent.

Or perhaps you feel stuck on a squad of limited abilities with a coach whose knowledge of the sport isn't adequate to meet your needs. If so, you have all the more reason to work doubly hard. Remember—lots of great players came from rough backgrounds.

By committing to excellence, you'll be amazed at what you can achieve. It's all about attitude and love for the game. You must try every bit as hard when your team is winning or losing big as you do when a game is on the line. You must train with the same intensity that you bring to a big game. And you must be willing to spend countless hours working with a ball while others are headed for the beach.

Still, the hard work in and of itself will be of limited value if it's not accompanied by an intelligent long-range plan that encompasses your becoming proficient at all aspects of the game. That's why I'll tell you what I did on my own to improve my first touch. You'll learn the shooting exercises that I performed religiously, which gave me the ability to score that goal in Trinidad. I'll describe my favorite games and drills and those of my fellow pros; all of these games, drills, and exercises you can do with just a few friends. Many you can do with a single partner. I'll also tell you how you can become a better player just by knowing what to look for while seated in a stadium.

Once you know what to do, being successful, like winning, all depends on your attitude. One tale that sums it up for me involved veteran coach Eddie Firmani. After several great seasons with the North American Soccer League's Tampa Bay Rowdies, he found himself laboring in the relative obscurity of the old American Soccer League. Accustomed to the big-time atmosphere, Firmani was taken aback one day when he requested a drink from a team attendant. Their conversation went something like this:

Firmani: What do you have?

Attendant: Dr. Pepper.

Firmani: What else?

Attendant: That's it.

Firmani: These cans are warm. Do you have any cold ones?

Attendant: No.

Firmani: Do you have any ice?

Attendant: Sorry.

At that point Firmani put his arm around the youngster's shoulders. "Son," offered Eddie in a fatherly manner, "just remember—it's the little things that win soccer games!"

It's doing the so-called little things to the best of your ability that helps you reach your goals. I believe this book will assist you in that regard. Good luck!

Paul Caligiuri

Acknowledgments

Paul Caligiuri: First and foremost, I thank my wife, Dawn Caligiuri, for her love, support, and patience, and for always being there for me—through the good times and the bad—on both home and foreign soil.

I doubt I would have made it in soccer were it not for the guidance and wisdom my father provided throughout my life. My biggest thank-you goes to him and his wife, Mona. I'd also like to thank my wife's parents, Robert and Judy Perkins, for their encouragement; my brother John for always being there to play soccer with me; my sisters, Roberta Steponovich, Lori Amthor-Martin, and Diane Pirozzi, for putting up with me; and my half-brother, Jim Ballard. Special thanks go to my children, Ashley and Kayley, for the inspiration they provide.

Without the care, direction, and supervision of many fine coaches, I would never have fulfilled my potential in soccer. Thanks to all of you, especially to Sigi Schmid and Steve Sampson for teaching me the importance of discipline and determination while I was at UCLA.

And, finally, thanks to the many American soccer pioneers who paved the way for my generation to have the opportunities that have been presented to us. I am grateful to our 1950 World Cup team for that marvelous 1-0 upset of England and to the many NASL coaches, players, and administrators who gave of themselves for the good of the game.

Dan Herbst: Thanks to my wife, Sandy Herbst, for her love, support, friendship, and understanding, and to my soccer-playing sons, Colin Herbst and Larry Antinozzi. I hope Colin and Larry find something in these pages to inspire them to take their games to the next level. Thanks to my father, Joseph Herbst, and his friend, Lois Cohen; to my sister Diana; and to Lou Gallo, a fantastic coach, teacher, and friend. I also offer a special tribute to the memory of a real mensch of a mom, Zelda Herbst.

We both would like to express our gratitude to Intersports' Cory Clemetson for his assistance and great advice; to all of our friends at Reebok, with a special thanks to Don Rawson; to editors Ken Mange and Marni Basic and the staff at Human Kinetics; and to Cobi Jones, a great teammate and a wonderful person. We wish to acknowledge the vital contributions of photographers Jon Van Woerden, Steve Slade, and Wilfried and Valeria Witters; Mike Herman of Yorktown One-Hour Photo; and all of those who participated in the photo shoots, with a special tip of the hat to an outstanding youth team, the Yorktown Cesars.

The Yorktown Cesars. *Front row (from left):* Ben Arnold, Craig Bergquist, Seth Intriligator, Scott Rodman, Brian Moorehouse, and Larry Antinozzi. *Back row:* Brendan Goodwin, Tommy Werney, Paul Chakmakjian, Danny Lenhardt, Michael Canniff, Amir Hammad, Kurt Thomas, Joe Parisi, and Michael Heady. *Not pictured:* Robbe Holiber.

CHAPTER
1

Living the Game

*"Make that soccer
ball your best friend."*

There's an old joke about a tourist who asks a native New Yorker, "How do I get to Carnegie Hall?" The New Yorker's response: "Practice, practice, practice."

To fulfill your potential as a soccer player involves an equally simple equation: How do you get to the World Cup? The answer: Play, play, and play some more. The more time you spend working purposefully with a ball, the better player you'll become.

Although in this chapter I do relate many experiences from my youth, I haven't done so just to reminisce about my childhood. It's my intention that you'll gain some insight into what you can do to become the best player you can be.

There's very little in my background that's unique among pro players. Yes, there are some players who are incredibly gifted athletes, but these are the minority. A far greater percentage of today's professionals owe their livelihood to an unbridled passion for the sport that drove them as kids to play at every opportunity. To excel at this game, you have to live and breathe soccer. You have to love the game. This is true for me. In fact, such is my love for soccer that even today, after thousands of hours with a soccer ball, I've lost none of my enthusiasm. I watch games whenever possible, even when the teams are at a level far below that at which I'm lucky enough to be competing. I not only enjoy watching, I always feel that I can learn something by doing so.

Living the game is important, particularly in our country, where most youth club teams train but one to three times a week and play one game on the weekend. Subtract the time required for stretching, water breaks, and instructions from the coach, and they're lucky if their total soccer time approaches five hours. That's nowhere near enough time to become a good soccer player. As a dedicated player, it's up to you to take the initiative to fill that void. I guarantee you that any pro you watch on TV or in a stadium was highly motivated to play soccer while a kid.

If you drive through any American inner city, you'll see groups of young people playing hoops at the playground. The winners stay on while losers wait around, hoping for another game. Competitive? You bet. It's no coincidence that a significant percentage of NBA stars trace their roots to the playgrounds. And it's no different with soccer—the best players are those with the most internal motivation. They fit soccer into their schedules, no matter what.

A PASSION TO PLAY

The United States 1990 and 1994 World Cup squads featured three starters who hailed from Kearny, New Jersey. How could it be that a town of 35,000 (about 1/7,500 of the U.S. population at the time) had developed over one-quarter of our lineup? How did John Harkes, Tab Ramos, and Tony Meola get to that level?

All three played for a strong club and scholastic team in a place that took its soccer very seriously. All are sons of working-class, first-generation Americans from Scotland, Uruguay, and Italy, respectively. Each of their dads had a passion for the world's most popular sport, which they passed on to their sons. It's no wonder that John, Tab, and Tony wanted to be involved with the sport during virtually every free moment.

To this day, John still talks about what a thrill it was to watch the famous New York Cosmos duo of Pele and Franz Beckenbauer in a packed Giants Stadium. For hours before the match, the parking lot

Fig. 1.1 Our starting squad against Switzerland in the 1994 World Cup—three are Kearny boys. Front row: Wynalda, Ramos, Harkes, Dooley, and me. Back row: Kooiman, Balboa, Lalas, Sorber, Stewart, and Meola.

was filled with youngsters like John kicking around soccer balls. Afterward, the Harkes family would return home, and John would rush outside to try a new move he'd seen that afternoon. His hours of soccer solitaire were interrupted only by trips inside to watch the sports report on the evening news to catch the Cosmos' highlights.

Kearny kids spent a lot of time at what's called The Courts in nearby Harrison. (You may recall seeing a shoe commercial that was filmed there.) As in playground basketball, the rules at The Courts called for the winners to stay on and the losers to wait. Teams usually consisted of four players. If it snowed, everyone brought a shovel to clear off the surface so the games could begin.

This passion to play is a common ingredient that runs through virtually every member of the U.S. National Team. Unlike John, Tab, and Tony, Alexi Lalas grew up far outside a soccer hotbed. He traveled hours to find games against older and better opponents. St. Louis product Mike Sorber hung around his dad's practices at St. Louis Community College at Florissant Valley. As a teen, he was known to entice some of the college players to cut class to play soccer with him. The informal "five-on-five" evening games in the school's gym saw Mike's team enjoy a numerical edge since he and his dad, the coach, officially counted as only one player!

Long before Joe-Max Moore produced one of the best strike rates in U.S. soccer history, he spent hour after hour working on his finishing skills. The tens of thousands of free kicks he attempted during training hours paid off when he curled a ball over a Mexican wall and just inside the near post in extra time to give the USA a 2-1 win in the Gold Medal match of the 1991 Pan-American Games. Only with true dedication can anyone hope to score four times in an international match, as Joe-Max did against El Salvador in 1993.

Frank Klopas, one of the United States' all-time leading scorers, told me of the time that he drove his dad's car 45 minutes in a midnight snowstorm to an indoor soccer practice. The kicker: The car's wipers didn't work, so Frank steered with his right hand while with his left he reached out the window to brush the snow off the windshield! Such passion is typical of all top-class soccer players I know.

I'm convinced that soccer is one of the most challenging sports on the planet for the obvious reason that, with the exception of goalkeepers, it requires you to control a moving object, without using your hands, while under the pressure of opponents—a very unnatural demand!

One reason that I'm able to meet that demand is that as a kid I was lucky enough to have a best friend who was *always* available to play and who *never* wanted to play another sport. My pal never had to leave early because his mom called him home for supper or because he had to do his homework. He was always dependable because he never got sick. You guessed it—my best friend was a soccer ball.

Making the ball your favorite playmate can transform you into an exceptional player even if you're not a naturally gifted athlete. Believe me, not every star is blessed with the extraordinary speed of Cobi Jones. Few are as powerful or as intelligent as Alexi Lalas. Not many have the agility of Tab Ramos. But nearly all of them have one thing in common—a deep-rooted love for the game.

Another edge is that, as I write this, virtually every athlete in the U.S. National Team player pool has either a father or an older brother with an extensive soccer background. Clearly, part of a player's love for the game is in his blood.

For me, I had my brother, John, who was born 16 months before I came along. We grew up with my parents in a four-bedroom home in Diamond Bar, California. As far as I was concerned, the most distinguishing characteristics of the house were the two-car garage door and the long, flat driveway. I can't even venture a guess as to how many hours John and I spent playing soccer together or the number of shots that ricocheted off that garage door. I do recall that the stucco above the garage was smashed on several occasions. My dad would ban us from playing on the driveway, only to come home from work to discover more damage. I suspect that he finally gave up because he knew it was a losing battle. He understood just how much we had grown to love the game. (If my dad can take any consolation, Klopas's father had it even worse. Frank's penchant for practicing his volleying resulted in his knocking off two garage doors in his dad's apartment building!)

When I wasn't playing with John, my neighborhood pal Peter Gonzales joined in. We'd play one-on-one for hours on end. We were very creative in making up our own games, which usually involved shooting on targets from far out. (Soccer-Golf was one of our favorites—more on that game in the next chapter.) The distance from the doors to the end of our driveway was approximately the depth of a penalty area. John, Peter, and I would take turns playing goal while the other(s) would shoot from the curb. Another piece of good fortune was that my road was a cul-de-sac, so there were few cars on our street, and we could hit long balls to each other. We invented a game

© Jon Van Woerden

Fig. 1.2. Marcelo Balboa, the first American to reach 100 caps, grew up in a soccer environment as the son of a former professional player.

where you earned a point if your opponent couldn't return the long ball on the first touch. The street's curbs served as our boundaries.

When neither John nor Peter was available, I would kick the ball around by myself on a large hill under the freeway. I'd kick the ball up the hill and practice my first touch when gravity brought the ball back to me. I would change the angle of the ball on my first touch and pass it back up the hill on the next touch. Or I'd strike the ball first time using the inside, outside, and the instep of my right and left foot.

When I wasn't on the hill, I stayed home and booted the ball off the garage doors for hours. Of course I didn't just kick the ball around aimlessly—there was always a purpose to my work. One day, for instance, I might play two-touch. Once again, I would change the angle of the incoming ball with my first touch and then aim for a specific panel on the door as I passed the ball. Sometimes I'd use but one touch.

There were scores of variations. I'd let the ball bounce and hit it on the short hop with a variety of foot surfaces. I'd shoot the ball hard, flick it up on its return, and volley it against the door. I'd juggle it a set number of times and hit it off the wall while trying to receive it again before it hit the pavement. My purpose was to create and assimilate as many variations of kicks and methods of controlling the ball as are required in a game.

© Steve Slade

Fig. 1.3.   All that you need to improve yourself is a ball and a wall.

Even in southern California the weatherman didn't always cooperate. John and I sometimes had to turn the long hallway outside our bedroom doors into a field. We would shut all the doors. My dad's door would be one goal and the stairs the other. Of course, we'd use a soft ball.

Sometimes I'd run around inside of our house and play wall passes off the furniture, walls, or, for special effect, one of my sisters as she sat on the floor. I distinctly remember one incident in which Roberta was so infuriated with me that she grabbed my ball, opened our front door, and booted it as far as she could down the street.

I got even. One subsequent evening I intentionally kept dribbling around Roberta as she was trying to watch TV. As I expected, she again grabbed my ball and headed for the front door. Only this time I locked her out! Not only did I make her retrieve the ball, I also refused to let her in until she promised that she would never take my ball away again.

LET THE GAME TEACH YOU

Playing on my own is hardly something that I invented. I suspect that long before the English Football Association drew up common rules there were people with the same enthusiasm for the sport that I have. One such person was the man who revolutionized the sweeper position by adding an attacking element to his role. To this day, Franz Beckenbauer remains one of the greatest players in the sport's history.

Franz was born in war-ravished Germany only months after his country had surrendered to the allies. Economic conditions were harsh, to say the least. Too poor to afford a soccer ball, Franz would often kick around a tennis ball. Learning to control an object that small made it far easier once he and his buddies finally scraped together enough change to buy a real ball. (I'm convinced that inferior equipment helps foster superior technique. That's a major reason why the poorest countries often produce the best players—coupled, of course, with the drive to succeed in a sport that is seen all over the world as a classic avenue for poor kids to escape poverty.)

Franz and his buddies played at every opportunity. Today we refer to those youth pick-up games as "street soccer." I find it amusing that some of the most highly paid coaching advisors who have been imported to the U.S. to "teach" us Americans about the game end up preaching the value of including some form of unstructured play in virtually every training session. They come all this way to tell us something that we already know—to let the game teach the players.

Which is exactly how it worked with me. Like kids in Europe and South America, my friends and I so loved soccer that we weren't content to limit ourselves to two practices a week. While attending Pomona's St. Joseph School, during virtually every recess we'd race outside onto a complex of four basketball courts. Behind the courts on the far side was a chain-link fence. On the side nearer the school was a large wall that guarded a pool. We marked the goals by putting paper cups into the fence and using chalk on the wall. Since our school

© Wilfried Witters/Hamburg

Fig. 1.4. Franz Beckenbauer graduated from street soccer to become a hero for the ages.

didn't offer soccer, there weren't any soccer balls around. Like Beckenbauer and his pals, we improvised. Some days we used a basketball. Other days we'd grab a water polo ball or one of those red, bouncy playground balls.

Our personal equipment was not much more sophisticated. Trust me—whoever invented soccer didn't intend it to be played in white shirts with collars, long black trousers, and dress shoes. (Actually, it's not the entire truth to say that we wore dress shirts. Despite school rules to the contrary, the nuns were sufficiently understanding to look the other way as we used shirts and skins as our teams' "uniforms.") Traction and ball control in such garb became quite tricky propositions. But, again like Beckenbauer, if we could control a bouncy ball while wearing inappropriate footwear on asphalt, we certainly would find it far less difficult to master a regulation ball on grass while wearing appropriate soccer shoes.

There was one technical demand that the conditions imposed that proved quite helpful. When playing across four hoop courts, it's a very good idea to dribble with your head up to prevent running full speed into one of the eight poles that support the baskets!

PLAYING UP
• •

Another useful aspect of our version of street soccer was that the kids in my grade were constantly challenging my older brother's classmates. Taking on athletes who were a year older than we were meant that we had to compensate for their superior speed and size by making the ball do the work. Besides, on asphalt you dribble at your peril (I can't tell you how many times I came home with holes in the knees of my pants). I'm convinced that there isn't a passing drill yet invented that is nearly as effective as playing against opponents who are athletically superior to you (but not so much so that you are unable to compete).

Tactics in those games weren't as sophisticated as those, say, of AC Milan or Bayern Munich. We had some pretty fair talent on our team and, in time, rudimentary forms of tactics evolved. Gary Ashley, a superb athlete, was the kid who we relied on to maintain possession. Our strongest guy, Anthony Sanchez, willed himself to overachieving. He was our best striker of a ball, so we found ways to take advantage of his scoring prowess.

My brother and his friends weren't too keen on losing to us little twerps. To avoid their vengeful and rigorous tackles, I came to appreciate the importance of using my teammates instead of trying to do too much on my own. That lesson helped me to develop earlier than many of my peers.

As much as I wanted to win, for me those games were all about having fun. Because there were no coaches worrying about players taking risks, I was free to experiment. It was on the playground that a player could attempt something as audacious as an outside-of-the-foot flick. I'm convinced that creativity cannot be taught, but its likelihood can be increased when a youngster is placed in the right environment. Street soccer is just such an environment.

You may or may not be able to organize games similar to what I'm describing. If the possibility exists, I certainly encourage you to try such games as frequently as possible. Don't be afraid to put yourself in difficult situations. When playing a pick-up game or practicing in the rain, I would wear tennis shoes instead of my cleats. And we picked out the section of the park that had the most puddles. Along with driving your parents crazy, you'll be faced with a far tougher technical challenge. Whenever possible, apply the Beckenbauer principle—difficult conditions beget superior skill.

• •

*D*ifficult conditions beget superior skill.

—*The Beckenbauer principle*

• •

Even if your house doesn't have a two-car garage like mine did, I'm sure you can find some other kind of suitable surface to kick balls against. The great thing about a garage or a wall is that it never passes judgment when you miskick. It never thinks that someone else should be starting in your place when your first touch is off. It never criticizes you for missing that open net that cost your team the game.

Because garage doors are so understanding, you're free to experiment to your heart's delight. I can't tell you how many times I stubbed my toe on our driveway while attempting shots with my left foot. But I can tell you how happy I am that I did because it was my best opportunity to develop my "other" foot—which allowed me to have the confidence and skill necessary to score on that 30-yard left-footed volley against Trinidad and Tobago that got us into the 1990 World Cup.

After that great win, a million thoughts raced through my mind. I remember flashing back to just how fate had conspired to introduce me to the game of soccer.

HOW I GOT INTO SOCCER

As kids, my brother and I played every sport imaginable, from baseball to football to roller hockey. One day, Jamie Morrison, a boy three years older than I who lived two doors down from us, ecstatically proclaimed that he had just joined a soccer team. At the dinner table that night, John and I hounded our dad to let us play soccer. The next day the three of us were at a local grocery store where the local chapter of the American Youth Soccer Organization (AYSO) was holding its sign-ups. Thus did my brother and I become members of the Mustangs.

About all that I knew of soccer at that point was that the idea was to kick the ball into the other team's goal. During my first practice, the coach, Len Meier, told us to get in line. I raced to the front. I was proud and happy to be first in line, and I listened intently as he told us that the drill was to dribble to a cone and back. Of course, the only dribbling I'd heard of you did with a basketball. I knew soccer was a kicking game, so I wondered why I was being told to bounce the ball with my hand. Luckily, before I got started on the drill, Coach Meier explained what dribbling was, thus saving me considerable embarrassment.

From day one, soccer was a great experience for me. I knew immediately I had found something that I loved. A lot of credit for providing me with such a positive introduction to the sport is owed to AYSO's fun-first, "everybody plays" philosophy.

I was a natural forward who led our team in scoring every year. It wasn't long before I drove my three older sisters crazy by constantly saying, "Pro Paul, Pro Paul, Pro Paul."

John and I helped lead our team to back-to-back championships. The third year the team needed a new coach, and who should volunteer but my dad. John and I were against it because we wanted a coach with an enormous soccer background, and my dad's only exposure to the game had been through our matches. We both assumed that we knew a lot more about soccer than he did.

However, Robert Caligiuri is a man who always does his best at whatever he attempts. He read books, learned drills, and asked questions of experienced coaches. And he did a pretty fine job in leading us to title number three. He proved that the prototypical American volunteer parent ought not be intimidated when trying to coach a sport that he or she has never played.

• • • • • • • • • • • • • **Me vs. We** • • • • • • • • • • • •

As a young teenager, there was one season when I took a stab at the "other" form of football. The gridiron games were in the morning, followed by soccer in the afternoon. Although I did quite well at football, one close call convinced me to become a single-sport guy.

Due to a scheduling quirk, one day there was just enough time between the end of my football game and the start of my soccer match for my dad to transport me from one to the other.

Unfortunately, we got lost on the way. I was crying hysterically because I didn't want to be late and miss the start of my match. As my dad rushed to get there, a policeman pulled him over.

Fortunately for my dad, the police officer saw me crying, asked what was happening, and decided not to issue my dad a ticket. As he let us off the hook, my dad asked for directions to the field. "It's one block that way," he answered!

We got to the match at least 45 minutes after the scheduled kickoff. Good fortune was on my side—the game had been delayed and hadn't begun yet when we arrived. But I realized right then just how much passion I had for soccer. That night, I asked my dad if I could quit football. He spoke of the importance of seeing through a commitment. So I fulfilled my obligation by playing out that football season before hanging up my helmet and shoulder pads.

I appreciate my dad's having taught me that lesson. Many kids put their own desires ahead of what's best for their team. Always remember that soccer, as with all other team sports, is about *we*. It should never be about *me*. If you always put your team's needs above your own, you'll be a more valued player than someone who has more talent but less unselfishness.

In 1986, I was faced with another tough decision—and I remembered my dad's advice. That year I was fortunate enough to be named as the only American player to participate in the 1986

FIFA World All-Star Game, which was held at the Rose Bowl. Of course, playing with the likes of Diego Maradona was a fantastic thrill in itself, but this game also opened up the European door for me. After the game, I received an offer to join Hamburg in the German Bundesliga (first division). Naturally, I was delighted at the offer; however, I had one year of eligibility remaining at UCLA.

What a decision! For as long as I could remember, I had dreamed of becoming a pro. Now here was an offer from a team that only three years before had won the European championship—if I turned it down, I might never have such an opportunity again.

As much as I wanted to say yes to Hamburg, I knew that I had a commitment to my UCLA teammates and to our coach, Sigi Schmid. I stayed on campus. As it turned out, the offer from Hamburg was still good the following year.

As much as I enjoyed my early soccer days, the better players dominated games with ease. If I was to progress, I needed a more challenging environment. Once again, I was lucky. George Ratajczak, whose son, Jeff, was by far the most skillful player in our league, decided to put together an all-star roster to become a travel team.

Mr. Ratajczak was an experienced soccer man. He had immigrated from East Germany after escaping from behind the Iron Curtain by leaping over the Berlin Wall. The players he selected became the Diamond Bar Kickers. We were a good team from day one, and we got even better our second season when Cle Kooiman joined the squad. As you probably know, Cle started the game against Switzerland for the USA in the 1994 World Cup. Also on that team was forward Jeff Hooker, who would become a star at UCLA before earning 14 full international caps for the U.S. from 1984 through 1987. Another member of the team, Rocky Crisp, went on to play in the Major Indoor Soccer League.

With so much talent married to good coaching, we won the 1978 Western Regional Championship. Although I have no idea about the standard of youth soccer elsewhere in the country at that time, I'm convinced the Diamond Bar Kickers would have breezed to a national title if there had been such a competition back then.

Our most memorable event was a three-week European excursion in which we advanced to the Final of Norway's Oslo Cup. There were 172 teams in our age group, and the championship game was played at the local stadium. Some 22,000 people filled the seats. The opposition was the youth side of Sao Paulo, one of the greatest professional clubs in Brazil. Although we lost 2-0, the match was an awesome experience I'll never forget.

Our next stop was Berlin, where our three games included a match against Hertha 03 Zehlendorf. Among the alumni of that club was future World Cup winner Pierre Littbarski. We held our own in West Germany. Best of all, some officials of Hertha 03 Zehlendorf expressed an interest in having me join their youth side. My dad and I struck a bargain—if I could get straight As in ninth grade, he would let me go. As it turned out, this would be the only time that I can recall when my dad went back on his word, but I have no complaints. I got all As except for one B, but he let me go anyway.

I came back to Germany in March of 1979 just after my 15th birthday. I lived with a German family, attended the John F. Kennedy School, which is an American school, and I trained four evenings a week with that club on a dirt field surrounded by high fences. Virtually every practice included a lot of 1-v-1 and 2-v-2 exercises in a confined space as well as ample shooting practice.

The German coaches were very big on attacking down the flanks and putting an early cross into the box. Forwards were taught how to attack the near and the far posts while the outside midfielders in their 4-4-2 formation, myself included, worked on whipping in our crosses.

I arrived very curious about whether I could measure up to local standards. I was pleasantly surprised to find that my ability was equal to theirs. The confidence I gained from that helped me a lot later, when I endeavored to become one of the first Americans to play professional soccer in Europe.

The soccer and the entire experience of living overseas were first-rate, but I was homesick. After six months, I returned to California to start my sophomore year of high school.

THE STADIUM AS A CLASSROOM

The NASL was at its peak, with the LA Aztecs featuring stars from all over the globe. My hero was Johan Cruyff, who to this day remains arguably the greatest midfielder to lace up a pair of boots. He was a soccer genius. He could envision three passes ahead, and he was magic with the ball. It was around his unique gifts that Dutch coach Rinus Michels revolutionized the sport by introducing "total football" during the 1974 World Cup.

That Holland team, dubbed "The Clockwork Orange," was among the most attractive sides ever. They went forward as a unit and everybody defended when the other team had the ball. Players constantly interchanged positions. Such was this team's influence that in the modern game, fullbacks like Germany's Andreas Brehme and Italy's Paolo Maldini are bona fide offensive weapons.

Observing Cruyff was like going to soccer grad school. As a card-carrying member of the Junior Aztecs I never missed a game. On one occasion, when the Aztecs took on the Portland Timbers, I served as a ballboy. On the field, I was impressed by how much talking the players did during the match, how fast the speed of play was, and how physical pro soccer could be. One couldn't readily notice these things from the stands.

Like John Harkes, I gained immeasurably by being a fan of the game. It's distressing to me when I come across a youngster with

© Wilfried Witters/Hamburg

Fig. 1.5. Although he didn't know it, the incomparable Cruyff, seen here playing against West Germany in the 1974 World Cup Final, was one of my most effective "coaches."

great soccer potential who doesn't share that passion. Kids who play soccer without having the desire to attend pro and college matches cheat themselves. They are inherently limited by never giving themselves the opportunity to emulate the game's top stars. Had I not seen a player like Cruyff close-up, I wouldn't have been able to become the player I am today.

Joe Griblin/© Columbus Crew/Major League Soccer

Fig. 1.6. How far you go in soccer is up to *you*. How hard do you want to work to develop your game?

There are so many little things you can learn by intently watching top-class matches in person. For me, the LA Coliseum and the Rose Bowl were oversized classrooms. I'd isolate on a striker to see how he worked off the ball to free himself of his marker. I noticed the angle at which the midfielders positioned themselves to maximize their vision when receiving a pass out of the back. I saw the way that weakside defenders pinched in to provide cover for their teammates. Your eyes, when properly trained on what to look for, can be every bit as valuable to you as a world-class coach. I urge you to watch as much soccer as possible. And watch *actively*—zoom in on specific technique and strategies you can bring to your own game.

> *Y*ou can learn many little things by watching top-class matches in person.

Young players today have a tool that wasn't available to my generation: the VCR. As you watch a game, be sure to also tape it. Later on, replay the game in slow motion to learn a new dribbling trick or to better understand why a goal was scored. Watch what players off the ball were doing as a play unfolded.

FINAL THOUGHTS

A recurring theme sounded by Coach Sigi Schmid to all of his UCLA players is that it's the athlete who is responsible for developing his or her own game. Ultimately, *you* will determine just how much progress you'll make. Believe me, you can go far by outworking others.

To a large extent, we're all products of our environment. If you're genuinely serious about fulfilling your potential as a soccer player, it's imperative that you frequently put yourself in an environment that's conducive to your development. Playing pick-up games and street soccer, watching the pros, working on your own, and, yes, daydreaming, are all essential ingredients that got me to where I am today.

In the pages ahead, I'll try to relay to you some of the steps I took to becoming a better player. Consider this book a tool—but, like a carpenter's hammer, it's up to the carpenter to use it well. You can use this book as a positive step toward becoming a great soccer player, or you can let it collect dust on a shelf. Always remember that it really is up to you.

CHAPTER 2

My Favorite Practice Games

"Constantly challenge yourself."

I'm often asked which soccer-related games I most enjoyed playing while I was growing up. The five that I've selected for this chapter were not only great games as a kid—I still enjoy playing them today. In fact, I bet you'll find that virtually every professional has the little kid in him come out when engaged in 5-v-2 or Soccer-Tennis.

SOCCER-TENNIS

I'm convinced that Sigi Schmid is addicted to Soccer-Tennis. After nearly every practice he puts his ball skills to the test. But as good as Schmid is at this game, he never could quite match Bora.

Soccer-Tennis is a fantastic game and a great way to develop your soccer skills and savvy. If you can picture playing volleyball on a tennis court without using your hands, you've got a good idea of how this game goes.

Although the game can be played one-on-one, teams generally consist of two or three players. We pros use a service box on either side of the net for our playing area (although for three-on-three you may want more space). We play in such a small area because it helps to improve our touches and, in the case of Bora, my former coach, it allowed him to avoid running a lot (he's a clever man who knows how

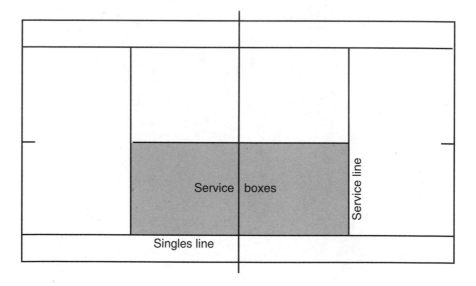

Fig. 2.1. Soccer-Tennis court. On the National Team, we use the service boxes (shaded area), or about the equivalent space, for our boundaries.

to modify the rules to accommodate his strengths while trying to camouflage his weaknesses!).

If you don't have access to tennis courts, use your imagination to come up with a substitute for a net. Benches work fine. In a gym, a rolled-up wrestling mat will do. If possible, make the top of the "net" about waist high. If necessary, lay down cones (or shirts) to indicate a neutral zone between the grids in which the ball may not land.

The action begins with a member of the serving team either drop-kicking or punting the ball into the opponents' side of the court. If you don't have a net that's at least waist high, you may want to include a rule that all serves must be lofted—otherwise the ball will be blasted into your zone.

Unlike tennis, there are no service faults allowed. If the serve lands out of bounds, the serve is lost. Do retake the serve, however, if it hits the net and then lands in bounds.

The receiving team may return the ball on their first, second, or third touch, but only after it has bounced first (this forces the receiver to move his or her feet, which requires that the first touch be executed while on the move). After the return, the ball may hit the ground only once after each time it crosses the net.

Fig. 2.2.   Soccer-Tennis is a favorite for players of all ages.

Since National Team players are accomplished jugglers, we don't allow anyone to have two consecutive touches. We also enforce a two-touch limit per team per return. You will want to modify these rules to best suit the skill levels of the players.

As long as the ball is in the air, it's in play. This means that if you kick the ball over a sideline it can be safely retrieved by you or a teammate before it lands. However, when returned, the ball must cross *over* (not go around) the net.

A point ends whenever the ball bounces twice, hits the ground after it's been touched by a player, is handled by any player, or isn't returned safely into the opponent's zone in three or fewer touches.

As in table tennis, after one side has served 5 consecutive points, the opponents then serve the next 5 points. Most games are played to 11 or 15 points, and you have to win by 2 or more points. You can play two out of three games or single elimination.

I know some Soccer-Tennis players who play that you can only score a point on your serve (if the receiving team wins a point, they then get the serve, as in volleyball). I don't endorse this approach, as it allows you the luxury of relaxing on your serve, knowing that a mistake will only cost you the serve and not a point. It's my philosophy that every action should have consequences and rewards.

So popular is Soccer-Tennis that it's not unusual for us to sneak into the trainer's room to play the game. After absconding a roll or two of athletic tape, we're ready to produce a makeshift net that extends from chair to chair or wall to wall. Although barefooted games in our locker room are quite common, I recommend that you wear indoor soccer shoes.

The more skillful the players, the more strategy comes into play. To watch a good game of Soccer-Tennis is to see the ball passed at angles with finishes varying from deft flicks over a foe positioned at the net to a header driven downward into the opponents' feet. It's hard not to appreciate the incredible skills of a Tab Ramos or a Claudio Reyna.

Each game that I've played has included a lot of laughter and good-natured kidding between teams. If you play with Bora, you also learn about the delicate art of negotiation.

CHIP-TO-GRID

• •

Chip-to-Grid is a fun variation of Soccer-Tennis. You use two grids whose size can be anywhere from 12-by-12 yards to 25-by-25 yards,

Fig. 2.3. The sharpness of Eric Wynalda's superb skills can be attributed to the fun games we pros play regularly.

depending on players' abilities and the number of participants. The grids should be separated by a neutral zone that can range from 10 to 30 yards.

As in Soccer-Tennis, teams generally consist of two or three players. One team serves the ball from their grid with a free kick taken from the ground. The receivers then have two touches to return the ball back into their opponent's grid. Unlike Soccer-Tennis, there are no restrictions on the ball touching the ground within your grid, as long as it doesn't stop.

The player who receives the long ball can either return it on the first touch or prepare it for a teammate. Both options require a high-quality touch. You may find that the two-touch restriction is too difficult for your current technical level. Should points rarely consist of long rallies, you may change the rules to permit the taking of a third touch. But try to play this game often enough that you improve both your long serving and your receiving so that you can progress to where all participants are comfortable with a two-touch limit. You can also play this game one-on-one. Scoring is the same as in Soccer-Tennis. Each side serves five consecutive serves before switching. Games are usually played to 11 or 15, and the winner must win by at least 2 points.

SOCCER-GOLF

I suggest trying Soccer-Golf if you want a game that's way above par for improving your ability to strike a dead ball. The idea is to get the ball in the "hole" in the least number of strokes (touches).

The hole can be anything. It can be a rectangular area marked by cones, corner flags, or shirts (using uneven terrain always adds to the fun). Or you can use a tree, goal post, or corner flag.

My friends and I often became quite creative when laying out our courses. We would play around jungle gyms, trees, and just about any other obstacle we could find. Holes with doglegs were popular (for you nongolfers, a "dogleg" refers to a fairway that has a sharp bend so that you can't see the green from the tee). We would play over such obstacles as hilly driveways or ponds (we had the common sense not to play in dangerous places, like streets!).

Soccer-Golf is a good game for improving your touch, requiring a certain amount of delicacy around the "greens." It's also good for working on putting swerve on the ball.

Part of your creativity involves coming up with restrictions that force you to become a well-rounded player. For example, you can play that you must alternate feet on successive shots. Or that only the outside of the feet may be used. If you're really ambitious, play that the final putt must leave the ground!

One of our favorite types of holes was to begin with the ball on the six-yard box. The ball then had to be chipped over the crossbar. If it went around the goal, the kicker had to use the following shot (or shots) to position the ball back in front of the goal. Another favorite was to set up a hole in a way that we had to swerve our drives around a corner flag.

Since Soccer-Golf involves striking long balls, make sure that you adequately stretch your major muscle groups in both of your legs before hitting the first "tee."

COMPETITIVE JUGGLING

Another great game is Competitive Juggling. Grab a few friends, form a circle, and one of you begins to juggle. The player with the ball calls out number "one," "two," or "three." The caller then flicks the ball upward toward another player. The receiver must then juggle the ball the exact number of times that was called out. As he or she is about to make the last touch, the current juggler calls out another number before passing the ball upward to someone else.

When a player fails to perform the correct number of touches, he or she is eliminated from the game. Players are also eliminated for passing a "hospital ball" rather than providing a serve that goes right to someone. Passed balls must always go higher than eye level.

© Steve Slade

Fig. 2.4. Group juggling can be done cooperatively or competitively.

A variation that allows players to stay in the game longer is to play H-O-R-S-E (just like the basketball game). For each failure, instead of being immediately eliminated, you simply gain a letter. You are not eliminated until you have earned that dreaded *E*.

Advanced players can add challenges to the game, such as playing the ball only with the nondominant side. On the National Team we'll put in a rule to restrict the use of a specific body part, such as "no heading." You'd be amazed at how challenging it is to receive a high ball when the most logical method isn't allowed.

Competitive Juggling can be played in pairs or with an entire team (a large group might play with two balls). It's a great game, so have fun!

5-v-2

· ·

As much as I've always loved Soccer-Tennis, 5-v-2 remains the filet mignon of all soccer games. I'd be shocked if there's a professional team anywhere on the globe that hasn't used this game on several occasions during the course of a season.

As you can guess from the game's name, it involves five attackers against two defenders. Players' skill levels determine how much space is required and/or if there's a limitation placed on touches. In the pros, we are allowed only one touch. This leads to players using a wide variety of flicks and freezing the defenders with some sort of deception prior to touching the ball while under pressure. Our grid is usually about 10-by-10 yards.

The standard format for this game is to play cutthroat. If either of the two defenders can so much as touch the ball, the offensive player who erred must go into the middle to replace one of the defenders. So, too, if the ball goes out of bounds. The defender who has been defending longer is the one to switch sides.

In the pros, we assign the two youngest players of the group to start as defenders, with the older of the two exiting at the first turnover. To add some spice to the game, we stipulate that any nutmeg calls for those defenders to stay in an extra turn. The rule when I played for St. Pauli in the German Bundesliga was even tougher. Anyone who was victimized by a "meg" had to donate 10 marks (about $7) to the Players' Pool. That fund became substantial by midseason. We used the fund for causes as diverse as paying for our team's Christmas party to helping out worthwhile charities. We considered any ball that went through a defender's legs to be a nutmeg, even if it didn't reach a teammate.

Fig. 2.5. 5-v-2 is the consummate training game.

In our games, when the ball leaves the grid, we are entitled to only one bounce before playing it back in (which is always tricky given that the defenders remain "live"). To balance that out, the attackers can keep the ball up with unlimited touches, but nobody is permitted to touch the ball consecutively.

There are also punishments for defenders (such as doing push-ups) for being so unlucky as to be in the middle when the 50th overall pass is struck.

A popular way for teams to play is to keep track of the number of consecutive passes and splits that are accomplished in a set time frame.

When playing 4-v-2, we allow every other player to use a second touch (if that player so chooses). At 8-v-2, it's mandatory two-touch. Slowing down the attacker forces that player to use ample pre-reception deception and to execute an excellent first touch. Because of the added players, we use a larger space.

I know of some youth teams that play games to 10 points. The two defenders are awarded a point for every touch of the ball and for any time that the ball exits from the grid. The attackers receive a point for a set number of consecutive passes (usually from four to seven, depending on the ability of the players) and 2 points for any split.

To play 5-v-2 well requires you to be able to make an accurate pass with a wide variety of surfaces while in tight space under the pressure of an opponent. It demands vision, quick thinking, and off-the-ball movement to provide immediate support for the player in possession. Having your body angled in an open position is necessary so that you always have at least two passing options available. It's also important to be prepared to receive a pass at any and all times, so you need to be on your toes.

Fig. 2.6. If you're going to play this hard in matches, you better play as hard in practice.

FINAL THOUGHTS

To be at your best in a match requires regular practice. Playing hard in practice games will carry over to how you play in real matches. One of the greatest selling points about soccer is that there are so many games to play to improve your techniques. The five games I've described in this chapter are as practical as they are fun—which is why we pros play them so much.

CHAPTER 3

Receiving

"Your first touch is your most important touch."

In a sport in which pundits and fans can seemingly debate almost any issue well into the night, there is nearly universal agreement that Brazil is the runaway leader when it comes to producing skillful players. It's not uncommon after a great goal is scored to hear a European television commentator remark, "You won't find better in Brazil."

The very first day that my former USA teammate Desmond Armstrong reported to practice at Santos, he discovered just *how* good the Brazilians are. The coach called the entire squad together. With his new teammates looking on, Des was handed a tennis ball and told to juggle it. At first he thought they were kidding. So they gave the ball to one of their veterans, who proceeded to keep it aloft using a wide variety of body parts with consummate ease.

Cobi Jones had a similar experience at Vasco da Gama when he arrived there in 1995. However, Cobi had an advantage over Des— he had been warned what to expect!

It might seem that juggling a tennis ball has little to do with playing soccer. But it does. If you can comfortably control an object that small, you'll have little trouble making a size five ball act on your command.

In a match, your first touch is the most important. If your first touch isn't sharp, odds are you won't get a second touch. Receiving a ball, especially under the pressure of opponents, is a vital technique. And the further you progress in the sport, the more important your receiving skills become. In fact, many higher-level coaches, when assessing players during a tryout, look for that characteristic before judging any other skill.

A good player consistently uses his or her first touch to escape from pressure situations. A very good player's first touch places him or her in position to put the opposing defense in jeopardy. A superstar like Maradona can receive a ball under pressure and instantly turn it into an attacking opportunity.

The next time you have the chance to watch a world-class player, hone in on how he receives a ball. Among the masters of the first touch are Italy's Roberto Baggio, Bulgaria's Hristo Stoichkov, Brazil's Bebeto, and Romania's Gheorghe Hagi. If you get the opportunity to see any of these players, make sure that you watch and learn.

Combining cleverness with a good first touch has allowed many a veteran player to extend his career. Owing to his incredible receiving ability, Franz Beckenbauer could probably still compete at a decent level today—and he was born in 1945!

• •

A good player is consistently able to use a first touch to escape from pressure situations.

• •

Such players with a great first touch always seem to have a greater comfort zone while in possession than do lesser skilled players. The primary reason is that they create a space for themselves that allows them to keep their head up on the subsequent touch. Moreover, they understand the difference between *real* pressure from a defender and what is often perceived as pressure by lesser players but which is not really pressure. I define "real" pressure as when that marker is so close to the ball that he can reach out with a foot to stab the ball away and/or execute a tackle. A foe who is more than two yards away from you should not cause you to panic. Simply move the ball to space and keep your head up. Don't hesitate to use the outside of your boots to pivot into the space that's behind you.

How often have we seen scholastic defenders sprint to a ball only to whack it into the shins of an onrushing opponent? If that's you, it's vital that you become comfortable at faking a kick, touching the ball to the side, and dancing around that charging foe. Of course, your comfort level shouldn't overshadow the match situation. It's great to be skillful and composed, but I'm also always cognizant of walking that fine line between being relaxed with the ball yet careful not to take silly risks in my own third of the field.

TECHNIQUES AND TACTICS OF RECEIVING

• •

There are several important factors in accepting the ball. The first is to know what you want to do with the ball *before* it arrives. It's imperative that you have assessed all of your options prior to executing your first touch. Even if on a high school or club level you've grown accustomed to getting away with failing to assess your options, be forewarned that you'll have far less time and space as you progress in the sport.

Your ability to see the field is especially important when receiving a square ball or a back pass. With rare exception, the reason your

© Jon Van Woerden

Fig. 3.1. By looking up, Thomas Dooley knows his options before receiving the ball.

teammate didn't attempt to penetrate the defense is because he saw that that there were several opponents between the ball and the goal. Had that not been the case, your teammate surely would have shot, dribbled ahead, or passed the ball forward.

In such a situation, you need to know how and where players are positioned on the far side of the field. You must know from where immediate defensive pressure will be forthcoming, as well as just how much time and space is at your disposal.

Your body should be angled so that you can see as much of the field and as many of the players as possible. That means that your shoulders ought not to be square to the incoming pass, or else your line of sight will be limited. Your head must swivel in an owl-like fashion so that you'll have "taken the picture" before gaining possession of the ball.

Having done that, you must now decide if the nearest defender is capable of immediately closing you down. If that's the case, it's imperative that you freeze the defender with a well-executed feint. When you watch top-class players closely, you'll notice how they buy themselves an extra yard or two by deceiving defenders before those defenders can close them down.

*T*o avoid negative results, "take the picture" before receiving the ball.

Your feint could be any of several movements. Sometimes you'll pull your leg back as if to kick the ball. Other times, a simple dipping of a shoulder can fool the defender and buy some time. Your feint could be a dramatic long step by your nonkicking foot in the opposite direction of where you'll redirect the ball. Or it might be to simply look one way and then go another. Similarly, you might begin moving one way before using the outside of your foot to go in the other direction. There are many, many different kinds of feints, and if you can get good at using several of them, you'll be able to keep defenders off balance.

When being closed by a player who is running at you, one option is to step forward with your nonkicking foot and allow the ball to pass by the ankle of that foot. Then, using the inside of your other foot with the toes pointed downward, cut the ball behind your supporting foot.

When showing for a pass in front of the ball (that is, when you're nearer to the opposing goal than the passer is), it's a good idea to try to make a bending run whenever possible. This allows you to receive the ball with your body in more of an open position (see figure 3.2). Once again, your vision is enhanced. But when receiving the ball under immediate pressure of an opponent, you must use your body as a shield and receive the ball with the foot that's farther from the defender.

Forwards are often called upon to hold off their marker while accepting a pass. This situation, similar to when a basketball player posts up, calls for leverage. Upper body strength can provide an important edge as you lean backward into your rival. Use your arms for balance and as a legal shield.

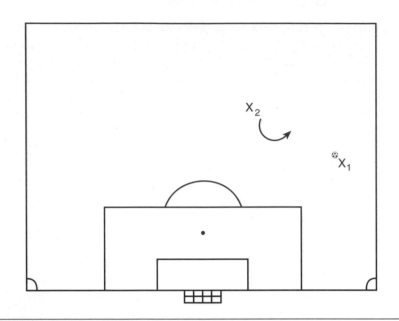

Fig. 3.2. By using a bending run, the potential receiver (X_2) of a pass from the player in possession (X_1) is able to read the game much better.

Your body is turned slightly sideways, and you receive the ball with the foot that's farther from the defender. It's quite a trick to negate an aggressive defender while keeping a moving ball under control with a delicate first touch. Later in this chapter we'll look at some practice exercises that help develop this skill. It is an aspect of the game that all forwards should master (it's also an important skill for midfielders).

Except for strikers and the occasional midfielder, most players receive most balls while facing ahead. As with virtually every soccer skill, your nonkicking foot is a key component. British coaches constantly implore their charges not to be "wooden soldiers" when receiving the ball. Being on your toes allows you to adjust your body to any deviation from the anticipated path of the ball. It also helps your muscles to be relaxed when making contact with the ball to provide it with a better cushion. As a general rule, you'll need to move to meet the ball; it's rare to be so open that you can wait for the ball to come to you. Upon receiving the ball, you have two options: to play the ball away with your only touch (see chapters 6 and 7 on passing and finishing) or to receive the ball as you prepare it for a subsequent touch. In the latter case, try to accept the ball with the body part that is closest to the ground (as this will take less time to control the ball

Fig. 3.3. Holding off a defender legally requires leverage, upper body strength, and first-rate ball skills.

on the ground for your subsequent touch). Accordingly, it's better to use your chest than your head, and your thigh rather than your chest. It's best of all to use your foot.

Whenever possible, present the widest available body surface to the ball. Using the inside of your foot gives you a greater margin for error than using your instep.

You'll notice that I haven't mentioned "trapping" the ball. That's because to trap a ball implies confinement. In the old days players were often taught to use the bottom of their feet to stop the ball. That concept is as outdated as black and white TV. Except for when you want to draw an opponent in to play behind him or her with a dribbling trick or to set him or her up for a wall pass, you must keep

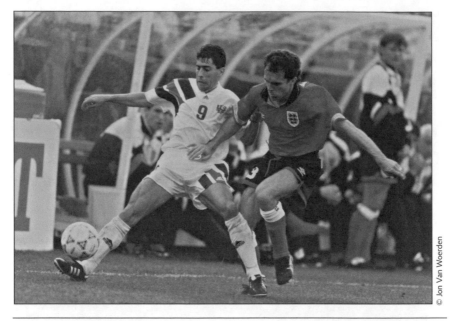

© Jon Van Woerden

Fig. 3.4. Tab Ramos illustrates how important it is for a midfielder to be able to receive the ball with the foot farther from the defender while holding off the defender.

the ball moving. Nine times out of ten, this involves altering the angle at which the ball has arrived.

When accepting a ball on the ground, bend the knee of the receiving leg so that the knee is closer than the foot to the direction in which you'll redirect the ball (see figure 3.5). This allows your foot to be properly positioned even if the ball takes a bad hop.

TRAINING ON YOUR OWN

Receiving a ball is one of the most essential skills in soccer. Fortunately, it is also one of the easiest skills to practice alone. All that's required is a ball, some space, and your imagination. There are dozens of dribbling moves, but most players can get by if they can master just a few.

In most cases, players have a dominant foot that they use to strike the vast majority of their shots and passes. However, with receiving, you can never dictate how and where the ball will arrive. As such, you must be proficient at accepting a ball with virtually every body part

© Steve Slade

Fig. 3.5. Bending your knee properly helps redirect the ball.

(except for your hands and arms), and you must be a two-sided player. As a kid, I spent hour after hour tossing balls up into the air and "catching" them with my head, chest, thighs, and feet. I would use the instep, the inside, and even the outside of both feet. I'd step one way and deflect the ball the other. Or I'd flick the ball over my head, pivot, and use a decisive first touch to move the ball away at speed.

Sometimes I'd work with a backboard, kicking balls at all different angles, speeds, and heights off the wall. It wasn't unusual that I'd spend over 30 minutes straight working on one specific type of first touch, such as to cut the ball with the inside of my left foot and take it away with my right. The key to such work is to make yourself play as if that wall is a live opponent. It's all too easy to fall into the trap

© Wilfried Witters/Hamburg

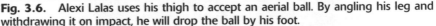

Fig. 3.6. Alexi Lalas uses his thigh to accept an aerial ball. By angling his leg and withdrawing it on impact, he will drop the ball by his foot.

of waiting for the ball to come to you or to back off that last half yard to avoid dealing with an awkward bounce. But, in a game, such luxuries don't often exist.

As you improve, make it a point to add some pretouch deception to your arsenal. And be sure that your second touch is every bit as gamelike and purposeful as was its predecessor. My work with a wall included different patterns of movements. Here are some patterns you might try:

- Receive the ball with your left thigh, take it away with the outside of your left foot, and pass it off the wall with your left foot.

- Receive the ball with your left thigh, take it away with the inside of your left foot, and pass it off the wall with your right foot.

- Receive the ball with your right thigh, take it away with the outside of your right foot, and pass it off the wall with your right foot.

- Receive the ball with your right thigh, take it away with the inside of your right foot, and pass it off the wall with your left foot.

- Receive the ball with your chest and volley it back with your right foot.

- Receive the ball with your chest and volley it back with your left foot.

You can also practice turning with the ball. Kick the ball off the barrier so that your first touch will be challenging. Move to meet the ball at speed. As you approach the ball sideways on, get in the habit of glancing backward over the shoulder closer to the opponent's goal (that is, the shoulder farther from the ball). It is important that obtaining vision during a game becomes habit.

Maintain a realistic environment by receiving the ball with the foot closer to the wall and with your arms extended to improve your balance. Practice turning with the inside and the outside of both feet. You can even use your thigh to do the same.

Fig. 3.7. Use alternate surfaces, such as the outside of both feet, to help gain mastery of the ball.

Juggling is another exercise that can significantly aid your receiving skills. Although juggling in and of itself isn't a match-related skill, the touch on the ball that you develop coupled with improvements in your balance and confidence will help make you a better player.

Yes, I heard the criticism from some prominent coaches a few years back that we had, at that time, become "a nation of jugglers." The implication was that while keeping a ball aloft for 500 touches or catching it on the back of your neck are nice feats, a lot of our best jugglers weren't very good players.

I don't recommend that you spend an excessive amount of time juggling. The best way to learn the game remains to play the game. But there are tangible benefits to juggling, especially if you use a variety to include different types of touches. Instead of just counting your consecutive touches, you might also juggle in patterns.

- Hit consecutive touches gently and the third one firmly; repeat the pattern of low-low-high, low-low-high. Do it with the same foot or by alternating feet. Do it using the insteps, the inside of the feet, or the outside of the feet (or any combination of these). You'll improve your ability to receive a high ball with your instep.

- Hit consecutive touches low-low-high and then take the ball away at speed (yet under control) as you receive the high ball.

- Alternate touches by going head-chest-thigh and back up to repeat the cycle. Around-the-world is right foot, right thigh, right shoulder, head, left shoulder, left thigh, left foot, and back again. This, too, can conclude with your taking the ball away with a decisive touch that allows you to attack a space.

- Juggle while seated. I spent many hours doing this, either with the same foot or while alternating feet. It can also be done progressively. Strike the ball once with your right foot and then once with your left; twice with the right and twice with the left; three times with the right and three times with the left; and so on. While on your butt, toss the ball up, kick it, and catch it. Or begin juggling seated and then stand up while maintaining control of the ball.

I'm sure there are 1,001 other possibilities that you and your friends can invent. Be creative during your practice time. Spend enough time juggling to develop a comfort level with the ball.

© Steve Slade

Fig. 3.8. Don't just sit there—juggle!

Remember—all the exercises I describe in this book can also be done with a smaller ball. After you're comfortable performing a skill with a regulation (size five) ball, try the same with a size four and then with a size three. And, before you venture to Brazil, you'd better perfect the same skill with a tennis ball!

TRAINING WITH A FRIEND

The obvious advantage of working with a partner is that one person can serve balls for the other to receive and return. Having a server is only of real value if that person makes a conscientious effort to provide quality balls for you to receive.

A common exercise that you've probably done in a formal training session has the server and receiver facing each other about five yards apart. Using two-handed, underhand deliveries, the server tosses the ball so that it may be accepted with a thigh and returned with a volley on the next touch. The latter can be done with either the instep (toe down) or the inside of the foot (concentrate on keeping your ankle locked with the toes pointed slightly upward).

If you're quite advanced, you can use the outside of your foot. The ball can be positioned by the first touch so that it's returned with a side volley, or it can be received with the left thigh and returned with the right foot (or vice versa). Balls may be returned with any surface

a

b

Fig. 3.9. Working with a partner, receive the ball with your thigh (a). Let the ball descend and then volley it back accurately with either your instep (b) or the inside of your foot. Advanced players may attempt outside-of-the-foot passes.

on the initial touch, or they can be flicked up with a foot and headed back to the server.

There are literally dozens of combinations that you can come up with. The one constant is to be on your toes and to really push yourself to excel. Challenge yourself by aiming the return pass to a specific target (for instance, if the server has a T-shirt with writing on it, you might try to place the ball at one specific letter).

You can work with a partner while stationary or with the server running forward as the active player retreats. Adding the back-pedaling motion helps keep you on your toes throughout; it also improves your balance and agility, as you'll need to alter your center of gravity so that you're moving forward as soon as the ball is served. An alternative is for the receiver to move forward as the server retreats, or for you to both move sideways.

*P*ractice doesn't make perfect—practice makes permanent.
—*Charles Hughes*

Working in pairs, you can play balls back and forth. For example, volley a pass to your partner who chests it down and returns it to your chest with a volley. This too can be done either while stationary or on the move. Vary the distance between you and your partner. You need to become comfortable at playing and receiving long balls (both on the ground and in the air). As you improve, make a run after passing the ball. This forces your partner to look up before accepting the ball and to change the ball's angle as it's received to prepare to return it on the next touch.

My brother John and I improved our first touch by passing the ball between ourselves. We used a wide variety of first-touch skills as if we were under the pressure of an opponent. Both of us always tried to heed the mantra of our club coach, George Ratajczak—that the essence of a player is to "control, look, pass, and move." Actually, *look* should both precede and follow *control*, stressing the importance of knowing your options.

RECEIVING GAMES

Soccer-Tennis, Chip-to-Grid, and the various juggling games are fantastic for improving your first touch. Here are some other possibilities:

- If you have six or more players, you can play a "condition game" such as two-touch soccer. In two-touch, all players are prohibited from making three consecutive contacts with the ball before it's touched by another player. Any violation results in an indirect free kick for the opposition. This stipulation forces players to work off the ball to get open, and it underscores the value of a great first touch. Professional squads sometimes play one-touch. If one-touch or two-touch are too demanding, try playing with a three-touch limit.

- One Touch-Multitouch is a similar game. In this game you must pass or shoot the ball on the first touch whenever you have received it from a teammate who has taken multiple touches. This simulates the rhythm of a match while involving a lot of movement off the ball. The player who attacks a space with several touches creates space in the area from which he or she came that can then be exploited when a deep-lying player makes a penetrating run (see figure 3.10).

The greatest value of One Touch-Multitouch is that it forces players in support positions to place themselves where they can see as much of the field as possible and where they can play a positive ball immediately. Thus, the player who supports too closely will find that the play breaks down. The athlete supporting from too great a distance will find it difficult to execute a penetrating pass, as the defense will have had time to recover because the ball will take too long to reach the supporting player.

Conversely, the player who supports at a proper distance and angle should be able to play a ball that puts the defense in immediate danger (see figure 3.11, p. 50).

- If you have an odd number of participants, make one of them a neutral player. That individual, who should wear a bright-colored shirt for easy identification, is always aligned with the team that has the ball. You can play straight soccer with only the neutral player's touches being restricted. Or, everyone else can play two- or three-touch with the neutral athlete having either a like amount or only one touch.

As with all small-sided games, it's important that the field size be appropriate for the number of participants and for their ability. As a

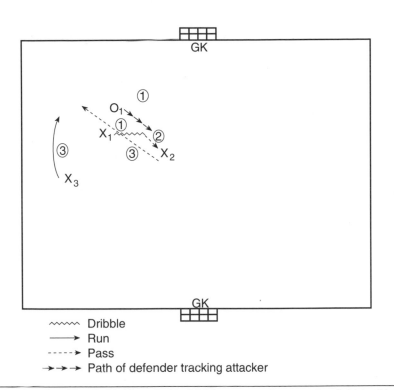

~~~~ Dribble
——▶ Run
----▶ Pass
➝➝➝ Path of defender tracking attacker

Fig. 3.10. One Touch-Multitouch. X_1 dribbles at speed across the field to "drag" marker O_1 along before laying the ball off to supporting attacker X_2. The space created down the flank by X_1's run can be exploited by X_2 with a first-touch ball into space for X_3 to run onto.

general rule, 4-v-4 to 6-v-6 requires an area that's 30 to 50 yards in length, with the width exceeding the length by about 10 to 15 yards.

Once again, good players can sharpen their skills by using a smaller ball, such as a size four or size three. But do this only if you're already reasonably proficient when using a size five. When working on my own, I would often use a mini-ball. Nowadays, most manufacturers sell good-quality mini-balls for about $10. I'm sure that using a smaller ball really helped improve my receiving skills.

FINAL THOUGHTS

Coach Ratajczak is right: The essence of soccer is to control, look, pass, and move. This is what all the great teams do so well and what allows them to make the game appear simple. Too often, however, club and

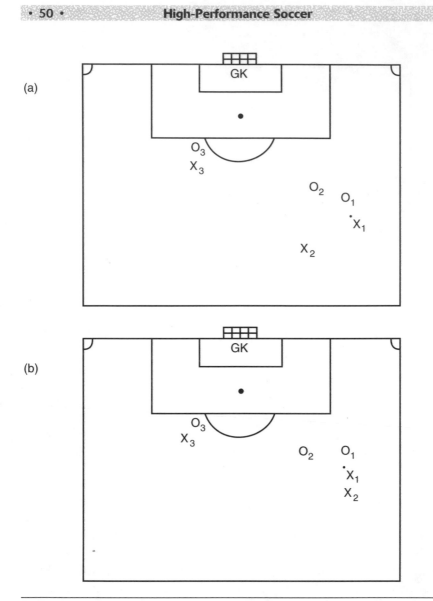

Fig. 3.11. Supporting at an inside angle and at a proper distance is vital. In (a), X_2 has three good options: to shoot after a good first touch, to change the point of attack, or play a penetrating pass back to X_1. In (b), X_2 has none of those options and will probably be closed down immediately after getting a back pass.

scholastic ball is "false." Because not every player is talented, a handful of athletes dominate. Those individuals can get into bad habits that will hurt them when they move to playing at a higher level.

*P*lay to the standards required at the level you desire to reach.

I know that I'm risking repeating myself, but I can't stress enough that you need to play to the standards required of the level of the sport you desire to reach. Don't let yourself accept the standards of the rest of the players on the field. The higher that you climb on soccer's ladder, the more important it will become to have a sharp first touch. I can't think of a single outstanding player who doesn't possess that quality.

Spend as much time as you can with that ball and with a wall and/or a few friends. Make a concerted effort to become two-footed. It's highly unlikely that I would have made the USA's 1994 World Cup team had I not done so. Today, my left foot is every bit as useful as my right (in fact, there are some people who think it's now my better foot). When Bora needed a left fullback, I became the logical choice.

Also, allow me to remind you again that whenever you train it's important for the skills you're working to be match realistic. Noted English coach Charles Hughes often notes that practice doesn't make perfect—practice makes *permanent*. By that, Hughes means that it's in training that you develop the habits, both good and bad, that will carry over into a match. The little things like being on your toes and taking the picture as you are ready to receive a ball must become second nature. This will only happen if you receive the ball in your backyard with the same urgency as you would in a game when you're being closed down by an opponent. Believe me, if you train smart, the skills you practice will carry over into games and make you a far more efficient player.

CHAPTER 4

Dribbling

"The most critical elements of dribbling are change of speed and change of direction."

Modern youth soccer has become more and more organized. I wouldn't be surprised if you, like many kids today, joined your first team before you entered grade school. Although giving North American youth an early start has helped the sport to grow, there has been one casualty: Much of soccer's spontaneity has been lost.

For reasons I can't fathom, far too many youth coaches today equate dribbling with selfishness. They ill-advisedly impose restrictions on their players that greatly hinder development. It's a problem that's not limited to our shores.

The one criticism of the contemporary game that's hard to refute is that there aren't many brilliant individualists who weave their magic a la George Best, Johan Cruyff, Charlie Cooke, or Pele. A significant part of the reason for this involves the evolution of defensive tactics designed to make certain that attackers are always outnumbered in the area that surrounds the ball and that their path to goal is constantly littered with bodies.

Because there's less space available for attackers, dribbling skill that helps you escape from tight situations is a vital offensive weapon that can create many opportunities for your team. And if you're a defender or a defensive midfielder, don't assume that dribbling is a skill reserved for those whose primary role is to attack. An increasingly popular tactic is for teams to apply high defensive pressure close to the other team's goal when there is an opponent (or opponents) susceptible to coughing up the ball under duress. As someone who usually plays in the back, I take pride in my ability to be able to dribble in order to maintain possession until a viable passing option presents itself.

But as much as team defending has improved, I think the biggest reason that great offensive dribblers have become an endangered species is the worldwide decrease in street soccer. It was on the cobblestones of the back streets of Europe and South America that the game's greatest stars honed the dribbling skills that make these players so dazzling to watch. Street soccer certainly promotes the development of individual skills in a way that organized youth soccer does not.

The good news is that dribbling seems to be enjoying a mild renaissance. Much of the credit belongs to an elderly Dutchman named Wiel Coerver, a highly successful pro coach whose teams regularly filled their trophy rooms. Only after he retired did he conclude that he really didn't know how to teach attacking soccer!

It was Coerver's conviction that the very essence of attractive and effective offensive play owes to individuals who possess the entire spectrum of technical expertise. Toward that end, he created what's known as the Coerver Method. You may know this method as the collection of "fast footwork" exercises that are now widely taught.

Unfortunately, Coerver's theories are not always accurately understood. Consequently, many U.S. coaches have criticized the method. Coach Coerver never contended that fast footwork alone could produce complete players. He's the first to concede that dribbling is only one aspect of the game. But he would quite rightly insist that it's a *vital* aspect that must be nurtured and encouraged.

If you don't know the Coerver Method, I recommend that you learn it. Check the references of the many camps that teach it; then select a camp that can show you a variety of exercises to do on your own (I'll offer a sampling of such exercises later in this chapter).

While we rarely see a brilliant solo dash like the one Diego Maradona had against England in 1986, the value of outstanding dribbling may actually be greater today because it's such a rare commodity. It's a fantastic offensive weapon that, when properly executed, wins championships. List the top players in the 1990s— Romario, Roberto Baggio, Hristo Stoichkov, Ryan Giggs, Gabriel Batistuta, and Mario Basler, to name a few—and you have cited men who are extraordinarily gifted dribblers. It's the same with the women's game. The dribbling abilities of Carin (Jennings) Gabarra and Mia Hamm played a huge role in the USA's capturing the 1991 world title.

Also, observe the comfort level that the vast majority of today's better American players have achieved with the ball. I don't think it was an accident that our coming of age as a National Team coincided with the emergence of several of our players as very effective dribblers. Whenever Cobi Jones flies down the flank, leaving defenders in his wake, it forces opposing central defenders to rotate. This, in turn, allows our most dangerous goal scorers a far greater opportunity to shine.

Midfielders Claudio Reyna and Tab Ramos are superior ball artisans. Although they rarely attempt to beat a succession of opponents, their dribbling allows them to escape from tight spaces and to create passing angles. Their uncanny knack for maintaining possession when outnumbered has not only reduced the number of costly turnovers, it has also allowed our team to attack far more effectively.

When Steve Sampson took over as coach of the National Team in the summer of 1995, he raised a lot of eyebrows by giving us the freedom to go forward as a team. That refreshing tactical approach

© Jon Van Woerden

Fig. 4.1. Tab's dribbling skills help unravel defenses—even defenses as strong as Italy's.

was an important factor in our winning the U.S. Cup and in defeating Argentina, Chile, and Mexico en route to a semifinal round berth in Copa America. But it was only because Steve was confident that his players could avoid being dispossessed that we could afford the luxury of sending so many men into advanced positions off the ball.

The backgrounds of Tab and Claudio reveal why they're so comfortable with a ball at their feet. Each played extensive street soccer while growing up in northern New Jersey. And both had a succession of coaches who encouraged them to dribble.

None of this means that you should be taking on three opponents while wide-open teammates are calling for a pass. But it does mean that you must gain the ability to beat opponents in the attacking third of the field when that's the best available option.

As with every other soccer technique, to be a good dribbler requires tactical awareness. It's essential that you always know where you are on the field as well as the placement of both your supporting teammates and the opposing defenders. With every touch, you must weigh the risks of losing the ball while dribbling versus the rewards of dribbling successfully. It doesn't take an Albert Einstein to calculate that your ratio of safety-to-risk depends a lot on how close you are to your own goal.

· ·

*B*eing a good dribbler requires tactical

awareness.

· ·

There are two distinct varieties of dribbling: (1) You can dribble to penetrate, where your objective is to get around defenders to advance toward their goal, or (2) you can dribble to maintain possession when the risk of trying to beat an opponent outweighs the potential reward and when no other viable alternative (such as an option to pass) exists. When in and around your own penalty area, it's foolish to be too adventurous. Instead, you should try to keep the ball until a teammate moves into a position where you can safely attempt a pass.

TECHNICAL KEYS OF DRIBBLING
FOR PENETRATION
· ·

Dribbling for penetration involves knowing how to best exploit angles to set up that marker. It requires deception and the ability to change direction and speed so that you can explode past your defender. Above all, what's needed is a can-do mentality coupled with a level of skill that can only be achieved by spending hundreds of hours a year working on your dribbling on your own.

Anything less just won't cut it. Here are a few keys for dribbling to penetrate:

1. Whenever possible, dribble diagonally instead of with your shoulders parallel to the goal line. This gives you more options and makes it tougher for your marker to stay between you and his goal.

2. Always keep the ball closer to yourself than to the nearest opponent. However, when speed dribbling, push the ball as far forward as you can without jeopardizing possession.

3. The two critical elements to beating defenders are *change of speed* and *change of direction*. Set up your moves by dribbling at less than full speed so that you can accelerate just as you change direction. As best you can, dribble with your head up and your knees fairly low to the ground. My boyhood hero, Johan Cruyff, might have had the greatest first two steps in the history of the sport. As soon as he would get a defender even leaning the wrong way, he would accelerate from first gear into overdrive. Trying to recover once he blew by you was like Wily Coyote trying to catch the Roadrunner.

Fig. 4.2. By quickly changing direction and then rapidly accelerating, I was able to beat this Guatemalan defender in a qualifying match for the 1990 World Cup.

4. When speed dribbling, contact the ball with your laces and with the knee of that foot above the ball. This will help you maintain control (even on bumpy fields) while allowing you to run at close to full speed.

5. Become comfortable performing a wide variety of feints to freeze and "wrong foot" defenders without your actually having to touch the ball.

6. If in doubt, be direct. The game's greatest rewards are reaped when you go to goal.

The Foundation for Dribbling for Penetration

First we should address power dribbling (or speed dribbling). With your emphasis on proper technique, use your shoelaces to dribble a ball in a *straight line* with the *same foot* as your toes point downward and slightly inward. Your objective is to be able to do this at close to full sprinting speed. Your number one priority is to advance the ball on a straight line. As you practice, it's preferable to virtually walk while keeping the ball on course than to move too fast and kick the ball every which way.

Once you have mastered this skill, you're ready to use it to set up a number of moves. Of these, the most basic is to dribble with your toes down and using the inside of the foot against the outside of the ball (or vice versa) to change its direction before you accelerate away from your marker. The beauty of this maneuver is its simplicity, the lack of technical demand placed on the attacker, and how difficult it is for a defender to read, as only a slight change of foot position is required to alter the ball's path.

You'll use the power dribble to set up many of your penetrating moves.

Six Basic Moves for Penetration

There are scores of moves designed to leave your opponent with a lovely view of your shoulder blades as you dance toward his or her goal. For simplicity's sake, I'll describe them as you'd perform them with your *right* foot. Just substitute the words "right" for "left" and "counterclockwise" for "clockwise" when performing the moves with your left foot.

1. Power dribble either up the wing or diagonally across the field at less than full speed. Pull your knee upward and use the bottom of

© Dan Herbst

Fig. 4.3. When speed dribbling, keep your knee over the ball and run with a natural stride.

your foot to stop the ball. As the defender brakes, push the ball forward at speed with your laces. The countermove is the old "hitch," in which you slow down and pretend to step on the ball with the bottom of your foot only to push it forward at speed.

2. Pull your leg back as if to attempt an instep kick. As the defender moves to block the ball, cut it across the front of your body with the inside of the foot (the right foot cutting the ball to your left).

3. When the marker is directly between you and the goal, fake a shot to freeze him or her. Then take the ball away using the inside or the outside of that foot, depending on the positioning of the nearest defender and on which direction will provide you with a better angle for a shot.

4. While power dribbling with your right foot, take a big step to your left with your left foot as you dip that shoulder to your left. Take the ball away in the opposite direction with the outside of your right foot.

5. As you power dribble at an opponent, bring your right foot behind and around the ball in a clockwise motion. Take a pronounced stride beyond the front of the ball to your right (toward the two-o'clock position), dipping your right shoulder to try to send the defender the wrong way. Rotate your left foot counterclockwise from behind the ball to its right side. With the toes of your left foot pointed downward, use the outside of that foot to push the ball away to your left (in a 10-o'clock to 11-o'clock position).

This maneuver, called the scissors, can also be done by alternating feet (the left foot moving around the back of the ball in a counterclockwise direction) until you have the defender wrong footed or backed up so far that you're in shooting range. As soon as the defender is wrong footed, use the outside of the *opposite* foot to take the ball away. For a reference point, watch USA midfielder Chris Henderson, as the scissors has long been his pet move.

6. Pull your right foot back as if to execute a push pass that appears to be aimed to your left (at about the 10:30 position). Use the bottom of your right shoe to roll the ball forward about a half yard. With your right foot on top of the ball, pull the ball back into your body. Turn your foot into an open position so that the inside of the shoe moves the ball to your right (to about a 1:30 position). This move, often called the V, was made famous by the great Hungarian star of the 1950s, Ferenc Puskas.

TECHNICAL KEYS OF DRIBBLING FOR POSSESSION

Possession dribbling requires shielding skills that include being able to use the outsides and soles of both feet to cut the ball behind your supporting foot without having to look at it. You also need a tactical awareness of where space exists and how best to exploit it. The general rule is that space is created in the area from which the ball has just come. Here are some pointers for dribbling for possession:

1. Use deception to buy additional space before being closed down by the nearest defender. Whenever possible, do not allow that

defender the luxury of getting so close to you that you must look at the ball.

2. Keep the ball moving.

3. Do not expose the ball to your marker. Keep your body between your opponent and the ball.

4. Only shield the ball when it's necessary. To maximize your options and your recognition of them, it's always preferable to face your defender and the play.

5. Legally use the arm that's nearer the defender for leverage, balance, and to keep that marker at bay.

Fig. 4.4. Excellent shielding technique—notice the attacker's low center of gravity, use of the arms, and how the ball is positioned to prevent a legal tackle.

Five Basic Moves for Possession

If you have attacked a space at speed only to be cut off, you almost always have the option of exploiting the vacuum that exists behind you. Keeping this in mind, here are several moves that take advantage of this principle:

1. The former Brazilian great Zico's trademark trick involving a stepover and a pivot is ideal when dribbling across the field or for a fullback racing back toward his own goal parallel to a touchline. (Just as an aside, soccer terminology commonly refers to a "touchline" rather than a sideline, and we speak of a player kicking a ball "into touch" instead of saying "out of bounds" because only when the ball is thrown back in is a non-goalie allowed to touch it.)

To execute Zico's stepover and pivot, pull your right foot back as if you're about to produce a push pass at a 45-degree angle to your left. Instead of passing the ball, step over and to the left of it with your toes pointed straight ahead. Turn your body clockwise and cut the ball with the instep of your left foot with your toes pointed downward. Now, accelerate to take the ball away at speed. Your first few steps are key. An initial explosion in the tradition of Cruyff will strand the defender.

Even though this move is often used by fullbacks, who pretend to pass back to their goalie before pivoting and dribbling forward, it is really not that risky because the body remains between the opponent and the ball at all times. However, remember that a smart foe won't be burned twice. If that player is on your outside shoulder (the one closer to the touchline) you are best advised to pass back, if that's a safe option, or to boot the ball into touch.

2. Cruyff's hallmark was to use a preparation touch as if to shoot or to pass long with his instep. As he pulled his kicking foot backward, the defender often lunged to block the ball. As soon as that defender dove in, Johan would point his toes downward and use the inside portion of his shoe to cut the ball behind his supporting leg. He used this move frequently to buy time and space for himself. Johan performed the move masterfully to freeze the nearest defender and prevent him from closing him down. For a more contemporary reference, watch Claudio Reyna, who also performs this maneuver adeptly.

As noted, you can also use this move to penetrate—it's especially effective when you're in shooting range. After wrong-footing the defender, you explode in the opposite direction on your next touch.

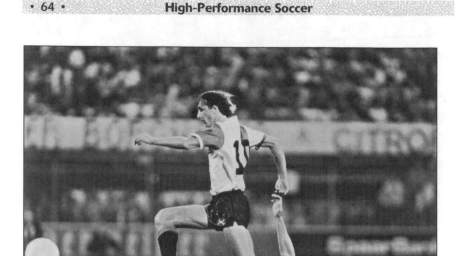

© Wilfried Witters/Hamburg

Fig. 4.5. After using his trademark ball cut, Cruyff explodes past his defender.

3. Quite often, inexperienced players lose the ball when a defender races from behind them to nip it away. Here's a move to try as an opponent is about to catch up to you. If the defender is coming from your left side, use the outside of your right foot to contact the ball at about 11 o'clock. Keeping your body between that opponent and the ball, turn with the ball in a clockwise direction using the outside of your right foot. Keep your toes pointed inward and downward. Use the part of your foot covered by the outside eyelets of your laces to touch the ball. One tactical tip—as you turn, look over your left shoulder so you're aware of the nearest defender's position.

4. As you're dribbling forward, if you find a defender is closing you down, step on the ball with the underside of your foot and pull it back toward your body. As you do so, alter the ball's angle so that it can be taken away on the next touch with a different foot surface.

5. There are several things you can do to freeze the nearest defender so that he or she will be unable to close you down. Fake an instep kick, step over the ball, and cut it with that same foot. Or take a big step to your left with your left foot (your supporting foot) as you dip your left shoulder, then take the ball away with the outside of

your right foot. Or you can step left with your left foot, bring your right foot over the ball from right to left, and take the ball away to your right with the outside of your right foot.

All possession moves require touch, talent, and composure. You must recognize the difference between genuine pressure (which might call for you to clear the ball into touch or far upfield) and what I call mirage pressure. Genuine pressure is when the nearest defender is within tackling distance (meaning that the ball can be contacted by that player without moving his or her supporting foot). Another example of real pressure is when the nearest defender is jockeying you to force you to move toward a covering defender who will be able to put in a challenge if you take another touch.

Inexperienced attackers often perceive themselves to be under more pressure than actually exists. Composure is a quality that takes time to acquire. Work to get to the point where you don't panic and

Fig. 4.6. Genuine pressure causes the attacker to lower his eyes to look at the ball.

clear the ball prematurely when you could do something far more constructive.

TRAINING ON YOUR OWN

As with receiving, dribbling naturally lends itself to training on your own or with just a few friends. There are also many enjoyable games and exercises focusing on dribbling skills that can be played by large groups of players.

Used as both a warm-up and a skill-builder, fast footwork drills provide you with frequent ball contacts while improving your fitness. Once you can execute the various exercises, challenge yourself by working with progressively smaller balls.

The first exercise involves ball taps. Alternate feet as you touch the top of the ball with the ball of one foot while hopping on the other. You should be able to develop a rhythm as you circle around the soccer ball without moving it and without having to look down at it. You can do this exercise with a partner, moving in tandem clockwise or counter-clockwise.

Next, use the front portion of the inside of your feet as you touch the ball back and forth between them. With your weight on the balls of your feet as you hop, you should be able to get the ball moving quickly. This can be done stationary or as you dribble around an area. If the latter, dribble for a set number of touches and then change the direction of the ball before taking it away at speed. The next progression is to "cap" the ball. As you're rapidly touching it back and forth between your feet, use the bottom of one foot to step on the center of the ball. Then quickly pull the ball sideways away from your body (the right foot pulling the ball to your right), as the inside of that foot moves to the outside of the ball. With the inside of that shoe, stop the ball on the proverbial dime. If you want, follow this with a capping move in which you cut the ball behind your supporting foot. Use the inside of your foot, pointing your toes downward.

If you cut the ball with your right foot behind your left, you should pivot counterclockwise and continue with the fast footwork (if using your left foot to cut the ball behind your right your body turns clockwise). You can also take the ball away at speed after having cut it behind your body.

Next come "pullbacks." With the ball in front of one of your feet, use the bottom of that shoe to pull the ball toward you. As you hop on your

© Dan Herbst

© Dan Herbst

Fig. 4.7. If you correctly execute your taps, the ball won't move.

supporting foot, the kicking foot moves rapidly so that it's behind the ball. Your toes point downward and inward to stop the ball with your laces—this helps get your knee over the ball for greater balance and control.

Pullbacks can also be done almost like a dance. While hopping on your supporting foot, push the ball away with your instep and return it with your sole. Perform several repetitions with one foot before working the other foot. You can also dribble in patterns while on the move. Alternate using the insides of either foot, then switch to using the outsides of your feet. Take turns using the inside and outside of the same foot. Alternate using the outsides of your feet (using the outside of your right to move the ball to your left and vice versa).

Fig. 4.8. Turn your foot inward and your toes slightly downward when capping the ball behind your supporting foot.

Also try dribbling around using only the bottoms of your shoes. Do this as you pull the ball with one foot while hopping backward on the other. Move to your left as your right foot comes across the top of the ball in a counterclockwise direction. Dribble forward with one foot while bouncing on the other. You can dribble normally before stopping the ball with the sole and then cutting it behind you. Pivot and take the ball away at speed in a different direction.

You can work on speed dribbling and changes of direction. Starting with a ball on the goal line, dribble to the 6-yard line and back. Then sprint to the penalty spot and back, the 18 and back, the penalty spot and back, and, finally, the 6-yard line and back. Also try creating your own patterns. Nobody says that they must be in straight lines. You can dribble to the penalty spot, back to the 6, and then to the corner flag. Be creative. Devise as many variations for these exercises as you can. The more you alter the exercises, the more fun they'll be, and the more likely you'll be ready to use just the right move in a game.

PRACTICE EXERCISES

Having worked on your bread-and-butter moves independently, here are some exercises that you can do with your buddies.

• Using any (and several) of the moves just described, you and your friends each dribble around inside a confined area (a penalty box or the center circle are popular options). Whenever you approach another player, change direction as you accelerate into space. Focus on using various surfaces to cut the ball.

• If you have a coach, parent, or spectator available, there are several good exercises that involve responding to a signal. Dribble inside the confined area. Upon hearing the signal, each player stops the ball with the bottom of the foot and races to another ball. The new ball is cut with the inside or the outside of either foot and is then taken away at speed. Also try this exercise using your knee to stop the ball. This is a good way to develop the feel for dribbling with your knees low to the ground, which was the secret of such players as Best and Maradona.

• Play one-on-one for a set time period (usually ranging from 30 to 60 seconds) in a grid about 10-by-10 yards. Play keep-away with the defender, keeping track of how many times he or she can either tackle away or steal the ball while the offensive player tries to maintain control. Have extra balls available to make the best use of your time.

• Another exercise designed to improve possession dribbling involves one attacker, one defender, one ball, and two cones (or saucers, flags, or shirts). Place the cones 6 to 10 yards apart, along a field line, if possible. On one side of that line is the offensive player with the ball. The defender is restricted to the opposite side of the line.

Using stepovers, feints, and ball cuts, the attacker attempts to dribble the ball to either of the two cones. The defender may not cross the line to tackle the ball. A challenge may only be attempted when the ball is within one yard of either cone.

The objective is for the attacker to wrong foot the defender. Having done so, the attacker then takes advantage by moving the ball rapidly toward the appropriate cone while maintaining full ball control. A "goal" is awarded for stopping the ball next to the cone with the bottom of the foot.

During the exercise, the offensive player should at no time turn his or her back to the marker. This exercise is a great way to work a variety of moves to freeze a defender and keep him at bay.

You can also go one-on-one in patterns where the attacker has a ball about 40 yards from goal, with the defender starting in his or her own penalty area. The defender moves forward to close down the offensive player, while the player with the ball tries to get beyond that marker to attempt a shot on goal. This can also be done with a server who rolls the ball into the attacker's path.

© Steve Slade

Fig. 4.9. Improve the speed and credibility of your feints by doing this practice exercise. Remember to never turn your back on the defender.

DRIBBLING GAMES

After a warm-up involving plenty of ball contact, try progressing to any of these dribbling games.

• As kids, we enjoyed playing what our coach called the Opposite Game. We'd dribble inside a confined area. To assure that we dribbled without looking at the ball, all of our coach's signals were nonverbal. If he pointed to our left we had to cut the ball to the right, and vice versa. If he pointed backward we had to dribble forward. You can play it Simon-Says–style, where the last player to react is eliminated. This game reinforces your ability to dribble without looking at the ball.

• Center Circle Kickout may be the most popular dribbling game in North America. Each player has a ball that he or she must keep in motion while maintaining possession within the center circle. The objective is to eliminate opponents by kicking their ball out of the circle until only the winner remains. You are also eliminated if you lose control of your ball and it completely crosses over the center circle line.

As with any soccer exercise, the size of the playing area should suit the number of players. When there are only five players remaining, use only half of the circle. Those who have already been knocked out can close in that half as others are sent packing. This game can also be played with teams consisting of two or three players each.

To add to the challenge while working on specific surfaces, play one round where you may only use the outside of your feet (or the inside or the bottom). In other rounds restrict all players to using their left or right foot only.

To add more fun to the game, reward those who tackle aggressively by saying that a player may return to the action when the person that eliminated him or her has also been knocked out. This will not only keep everyone interested and involved, it also means that to win you'll have to eliminate everyone else, so you can't hide as others are aggressively taking risks.

A third option promotes quick transition and what coaches call immediate chase (the idea being to get back on defense immediately after the ball is lost). If your ball is kicked out of the circle, you can remain "live" if you can retrieve it before it stops rolling and then sprint back into the circle before any of the other players have had their balls cleared.

© Steve Slade

Fig. 4.10. Center Circle Kickout demands matchlike decision making and technical abiilty.

• In one of the better dribbling games, you set up five goals along the center circle, each about two yards wide and with equal distance between them. Two groups of players are inside the circle.

Each player on the offense has his or her own ball. The defensive players each mark one specific attacker and may attempt to tackle only that player.

Within a set time period (usually 60 seconds), each of the attackers tries to score as many goals as possible. This is done by dribbling the ball to any of the five goals and stopping the ball on the line. Attackers are prohibited from exiting the circle. Should an attacker lose possession, the ball is returned immediately. As with the tactical demands of a real game, this exercise requires the players in possession to recognize space. Shielding skills come into play. Once an attacker changes direction, he or she will have to accelerate rapidly to score before the defender can recover. However, if a marker gets back into position, the attacker can just cut the ball again to keep his or her body between the ball and the marker.

For added fun, keep track of who scores the most goals and which defender allows the least.

• Using corner flags (or saucers, cones, or shirts) for goals, play one-on-one on a field that's 15 to 25 yards long. Place the "goalposts" about 5 to 10 feet apart.

A similar game is known as Winterbottoms. Once again, it's a one-on-one situation with players attempting to score a goal. In this game, spare players serve as the goals by standing at either end with their legs spread wide apart. Each is holding an extra ball in case the game ball is kicked out of play. When that happens, the person serving as the goal drops the ball at the feet of the player who is attacking the far goal. However, before this occurs, the opposing player is allowed to recover to get on goalside, thus forcing the attacker to use a dribbling trick to get around the defender.

In consideration of the friends who serve as goalposts, a goal may only be scored if the ball is rolled. Some players, especially the males, aren't too fond of shots that leave the turf!

You can also play this game 1-v-1 with big goals guarded by keepers. This variation not only helps the attacker but also teaches the player without the ball to jockey as he or she tries to force the offensive player onto the weaker foot and away from the goal.

• A team game designed to force you to dribble for penetration involves playing regular soccer with the proviso that you may not pass the ball forward or square. Another way to play is to enforce a minimum number of touches. As opposed to playing one-touch or two-touch to improve passing skills and off-of-the-ball movements, minimum-touch requires you to dribble effectively and attack a space (if you don't, you'll quickly be surrounded by a posse of defenders). I recommend playing either a four- or a five-touch minimum. In other words, each time that a player receives the ball he or she must touch the ball at least that number of times before passing or shooting. If the minimum number of touches isn't made, the defending team is awarded an indirect free kick from the spot of the "foul."

• A dribbling game that incorporates tackling, finishing, fitness, and some tactical demands is 1-v-1-v-1. Divide your friends into three equal teams and play on a field about 20 to 30 yards long. A keeper guards each of the regulation-sized goals on the endlines.

All three teams send out one player for a 60-second period. A ball is served into the area, with each athlete attempting to score on either goal. A new ball is sent into play whenever the old one leaves the playing area or a keeper gains possession. After time expires, another three players take their turn. The first team to score a set number of goals is the winner.

DEFENDING AGAINST THE DRIBBLE
• •

As you might expect, during practice, the better the defensive players defend, the better the offensive players will become. And of course, with rare exceptions, during a game you must be a two-way player to succeed in this sport. Thus, you need to practice your defense as well as your offense. Here are some tips on defending against the dribble.

1. When defending the dribble, keep your eyes riveted to the ball. Your weight should be on the balls of your feet as you bend from your knees and your waist. Maintain your balance at all times.

2. Move as quickly as you can to the player in possession of the ball. The denial of time and space is an essential element of defense.

3. As you approach the player in possession, get close enough to bring his or her head down. This usually means getting within a few yards of the ball. However, never charge in like a bull or the attacker will tap the ball to the side and dance around you. As you get near an opponent, slow down and begin to backpedal at about the same speed as the player is running forward.

4. Keep your feet about shoulder-width apart and your knees bent. Maintaining a low center of gravity and good balance is necessary for you to be able to change direction as quickly as can the player with the ball.

5. Angle yourself so that one foot is closer to the opponent. As you approach, try to force him or her to go in the direction that is less dangerous to your team. Known as *jockeying, forcing,* or *funneling* an opponent, this technique is important in that it allows your teammates behind you to assume good covering positions.

6. Be patient. Let the attacker initiate the movements. The only time you'll make a move is to use your shoulders to fake a tackle when trying to make the opponent panic and mistouch the ball. Usually you should only try a tackle when you're confident of winning the ball. When you do take a chance on a tackle you're not sure of, make certain you're in the attacking third of the field or that teammates are covering for you.

Fig. 4.11. Only launch a tackle when you're confident you'll win the ball or if you're in a desperate situation.

FINAL THOUGHTS

When it comes to dribbling skills, you can also let your television coach you. Put your VCR to good use the next time there's a top-class match on the tube. Unless you have a four-head recorder, be sure to tape on the six-hour speed mode so that you can review the action in slow motion. Whenever a player performs an effective dribbling maneuver, make a note of what he or she did, in what situation the move was used, and why it worked. Then go out in the backyard and try the move yourself.

As they say of snowflakes, no two soccer players dribble exactly alike. Some of us are short, some tall, and some (like me) in between. Some players have big feet, others small feet, and some (again like me) in between. Some are highly flexible while others aren't so gifted. Regardless of your natural ability, try to feel comfortable while you're dribbling.

No matter how you get the job done, it's important that you learn to dribble well so that you don't panic when a ball is played to you. Without exception, every top-level player I've played with could dribble at least competently. Even a tall central defender who rarely dribbles must be able to dribble when called upon.

Virtually all good players are good dribblers who do one or two things exceptionally well. My USA teammates through the years all have a trademark move with which they have been able to beat opponents.

Frank Klopas's forte is using the inside and outside of either foot while power dribbling at speed. He's great at cutting sharply while

Fig. 4.12. With very rare exception, all good attacking players are proficient dribblers who have a pet move and an effective countermove.

keeping the ball close to his foot. Roy Wegerle opens his hips as if to pass to his right with his right foot only to use the inside of that foot to curl the ball across his body (this is also the pet move of Brazil's Romario). Cobi Jones makes use of his greatest asset, his speed. He runs at angles rapidly before slowing down. The defender must do the same. It's then that Cobi fires up the jets as he rockets past his helpless marker. So effective is he that opposing defenses know to get a covering defender in position behind his marker. Opponents are in constant fear of being caught facing him one-on-one, where there's space behind the defender for Cobi to exploit. Joe-Max Moore dips his left shoulder to wrong foot his marker before taking the ball away with the outside of his right foot. John Harkes seems to expose the ball to his defender, only to pull it away at speed before the defender can come in. Tab Ramos is a master at getting his marker to bite. He'll often look away while dribbling to fool his defender into thinking that he doesn't know he's there. Then he'll dash away the second that the marker lunges into a tackle.

*V**irtually all good players are good dribblers who do one or two things exceptionally well.*

Me? I'm not too flashy, but I like to fake a long kick and cut the ball (which is how I set up my goal against Trinidad in 1989). My greatest asset is that I'm just as comfortable dribbling to my left as I am to my right.

Other than scoring a goal, there's no aspect of the game that's more fun than to dribble around an opponent or two. Great dribblers have the ability to break down the best defenses. That's why a Paul Gascoigne is such a treasured commodity.

Spend the time it takes to get good at dribbling. Don't be afraid to take calculated risks in matches. And try your tricks against older players in street soccer until you possess the sharpness you'll need to pull off such maneuvers when you progress to the next level of the sport.

CHAPTER 5

Heading

*"Take pride in winning those
one-on-one battles."*

Because heading is a technique rarely used in youth games, you probably played for several seasons before you began to appreciate its importance. If you're like most high school players, the technique is not your strong suit. If that's the case, and if you're a defender or a forward, there is some urgency to improve. You must become proficient at heading to successfully compete in college or the pros.

Even if you're a midfielder or a goalie, you should become at least competent in the air. More than once this past season our keeper saved the day by racing out of his penalty area to head the ball away from an onrushing opposing striker.

I would also suggest closely observing how we professional players use our hands, arms, and bodies to gain leverage without fouling our opponents. As with most team sports, soccer isn't played by a literal interpretation of the rules. Instead, a liberal amount of contact is expected by college and pro players and permitted by referees. Thus, strength is just as important a factor to getting your head to the ball as are your sense of anticipation, size, timing, and jumping ability. Very few college freshmen win aerial duels against older, bigger, stronger, and more experienced foes. My advice to the campus-bound is to spend considerable time working on various heading techniques and to start a weight-training program before your senior year in high school. I recommend a program designed to improve your upper body strength and add to your vertical jump. Consult a qualified instructor on how to best proceed.

TECHNICAL KEYS OF HEADING

Several technical factors come into play for heading a ball with power and accuracy:

1. Keep your eyes open and your mouth closed. Your eyes will automatically blink on impact, but a good trick is to constantly remind yourself to "throw" your eyes at the ball.

2. Contact the ball just underneath your hairline, either on the center of your forehead or on that hard bone above the outside edge of either eyebrow.

3. Keep your neck locked (except when you're performing a flick-on header).

4. Thrust your upper body forward to provide added power.

5. Use your arms to increase your balance and, when necessary, to subtly impede an opponent.

6. Time your jump so that you head the ball during the highest point of your leap.

Fig. 5.1. High-scoring USA striker Michelle Akers gains the maximum edge on her Canadian opponent by making contact at the highest point of her leap.

7. When clearing a ball with a defensive header, hit just under the center of the ball. Your top priorities, in order, are to obtain height, width, and distance.

8. A strike on goal usually calls for heading the ball downward. When doing so, contact the top half of the ball. In most cases you want the ball to hit the ground just as it's passing by the keeper, as this is the most difficult save to make. When in doubt, head the ball back toward the post in the same direction from where the cross originated.

9. Be fearless. We're all concerned about clashing heads with an opponent, but that's no excuse for a half-hearted effort. To head a ball requires an all-out commitment. Technique without courage is like a race car without gasoline.

10. Take pride in winning those one-on-one battles. Determination counts for a lot. I'm not particularly big, but I held my own in the Bundesliga and in internationals against forwards well over six feet tall. Had I not been able to do so, I would never have played at such a high level for so long (if at all). And I certainly wouldn't have ever been used in a central defensive position.

PRACTICE EXERCISES

When designing your training, the variations you practice should include all those that you might have to try in matches. Some of these are not easy to duplicate, especially if you're working on your own or with only a friend or two. Round up a few pals and design your own heading training session.

• For a warm-up, you and a friend can head the ball back and forth. Keep track of how many consecutive touches you can do. As kids, my friends and I were forever trying to top our own and each other's personal records.

• As with all forms of juggling, you may also engage in patterns. Head the ball upward on your first touch and then nod it to your partner on the next touch. Your partner then heads the ball upward on his or her first touch and back to you with the second touch. This time you head the ball upward twice and return it on the third touch.

Fig. 5.2. Challenge yourself to set new records while head juggling with a partner. Keep your knees bent and be on your toes to soften your first touch.

Your partner does the same. Progress upward a touch at a time until you have reached 10 touches each. Then work your way back down to 2 touches.

• You can also train while taking turns being the server. Face each other from a distance of about five yards. The active player backpedals while the server jogs forward, holding a ball. The server throws the ball up high and slightly in front of his or her partner. The active player must jump and thrust forward from the waist to head the ball powerfully into the server's hands. This exercise can also be done with the server backpedaling while the active player jogs forward.

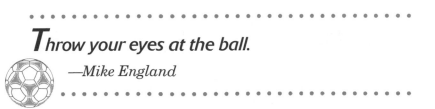

Throw your eyes at the ball.

—Mike England

• I believe that my jumping ability was improved by lying on my stomach. Upon the signal of my partner, I'd leap to my feet and then jump up to head a ball that he served to me. I'd then return to my stomach and repeat the procedure several times. I would also do this while working on diving headers.

• There are several exercises that you can do with three players. Place the active player in the middle, with the other two acting as servers. The active player runs toward one of the servers, who throws the ball upward. The active player leaps and thrusts powerfully forward to head the ball back to that server. Having done so, he pivots and sprints toward the other server and repeats the action. Also use this exercise to work on heading for distance or diving headers.

• An alternative is to engage in heading exercises with passive resistance. As shown below, the server tosses the ball over the defender's head. The player in the back leaps over his marker to head the ball forcefully back to the server. In this exercise you should turn your body so that you're sideways to the ball. Because your shoulder is nearer to the opponent than your head is, you're far less likely to clash heads. Strike the ball with the part of your forehead directly above the outside edge of your eyebrow. Failing to use this technique

© Steve Slade

Fig. 5.3.   Enhance your defensive heading by contacting the bottom half of the ball. Note that the active player is square to the ball because he's not near the passive opponent. If he were closer to that player, his body and head should be turned sideways.

greatly increases the chances that your nose will slam into the back of your opponent's skull, which is never a pleasant experience. The sideways motion also allows for greater freedom of movement of your waist, which provides power to head the ball farther upfield.

• Obviously, almost any heading exercise can be altered so that you can shoot on goal. Try this one to work on offensive and defensive heading. You and a partner stand on the six-yard line, facing each other. Head juggle a set number of times and then try to jump up and head the ball far over the crossbar. Or head it powerfully and downward on goal.

No partner? There's always a wall that's willing to work with you. See how many consecutive times you can head the ball off the wall. Or how many times you can use a set number of touches, play it off the wall, and then use that same number of touches again. To work

© Steve Slade

Fig. 5.4. Enlist the help of your friend the wall for heading training.

on your defensive heading, head the ball upward off the wall. To simulate a shot on goal, toss the ball firmly off the wall, leap upward, and head the ball downward toward an imaginary goal.

Given that a big part of heading is beating an opponent to the ball, it's advisable to include jumping exercises in your training. As a boy, I'd run side to side and then jump up, thrusting off my left foot, right foot, or both feet simultaneously. I'd do the same after backpedaling or after having run forward. I know many players who either train on sand or use ankle weights to add a precious inch or two to their vertical jump.

HEADING GAMES

Here are five games to improve your heading ability while providing great enjoyment in a competitive setting.

• Who says that basketball players deserve exclusive use of a hoop and backboard? Soccer players can also play H-O-R-S-E. Instead of shooting a basketball with our hands, we'll toss a soccer ball upward and head it at the rim. Any shot that touches iron counts as a basket. Just as a hoop player in a game of Horse can call a "swish," you may call a "basket" (meaning that the ball must actually go through the rim to count).

You can also do ball tricks, as long as you announce them in advance. For example, juggle three times with your feet, flick the ball upward, and head it toward the rim. Or start with your back to the basket before juggling, flicking, pivoting, and heading. Or head juggle off the backboard a set number of times before trying to nod the ball through the hoop.

• The rules of Soccer-Tennis can be modified to focus on heading. Award two points for any header that can't be returned. Or include a rule that all balls must be headed across the net. You could also try using a raised net such as a volleyball net, but I prefer a net at chest-high level, as this allows you to drive the ball downward as you normally would when heading on goal.

• To improve both crossing and heading, try a game that requires at least six players (a server, goalkeeper, and four competitors) as well as a full-sized goal (or the equivalent thereof). The server, with several balls, is positioned just inside the touchline and about 15 to 25 yards from the goal line. Inside the penalty area are two teams with two players apiece.

The server touches a ball forward, looks up, and then delivers a cross. All the players attempt to score. The team with more goals following a predesignated number of crosses (usually 10) is the winner. You can also emphasize heading by counting any headed score as two goals and any header that results in either a goalkeeper save or a deflection off the post or crossbar as one goal.

If you have more than six players, try positioning a second server on the opposite flank. Have the two servers alternate crosses. Eight or more players? Set up a tournament where the losing team comes off while the victors stay on. The team that plays in the most games is the champion.

• Play 3-v-3 up to 6-v-6 with neutral players who serve balls in from the flanks. The playing surface ranges from 30 to 50 yards long with normal (60 to 70 yards) width. Use saucers or shirts to mark off two neutral zones that extend 10 yards in from the touchlines. In each of those zones is one neutral player (see figure 5.5). Only these neutral players are permitted in their zones, and these two athletes are always aligned with whichever team has the ball. This game is played just like regular soccer but with a few twists:

1. The neutral players are restricted to either two or three touches (your choice) and must receive and play a ball at normal match speed. Forcing them to do this prevents a potentially false situation created by not allowing any defenders to challenge them.

2. The neutral players must prepare the ball and put a cross into the penalty area. They may not leave their zone, nor are they permitted to shoot on goal.

3. Because the objective is to upgrade your heading abilities, all goals scored on headers count double, whereas any headed shot that either forces a save or hits the woodwork counts as one goal.

4. So that the penalty area doesn't resemble Grand Central Station at rush hour (which would make getting a clean header very difficult), restrict the movement of players whenever there are more than three outfield players per team.

    Let's say that you're playing 4-v-4. At all times, each team must have two defenders on its half of the midfield line with two forwards in the attacking half of the field. The lone exception can be that whenever a cross is about to be struck, one of the withdrawn players on the attacking team is permitted to make a run into the attacking half of the field. Doing this allows the attackers a three-on-two advantage. However, should the play break down, either the defender who pushed forward or one of the two strikers must drop back into his defending zone.

5. If you're looking for maximum repetitions, allow the goal-keepers to throw the ball directly to either of the neutral players.

There are tactical considerations in this game that mirror those of an actual match. First, the timing of runs is important. The signal to begin a run is after the neutral player in possession has prepared the ball to be crossed (by touching it inward) and has glanced upward to survey the field.

Remember this simple rule: Your feet get on track only after making eye contact. All runs should be diagonal. It's very difficult to score on a header when your shoulders are parallel to the goal line as you're running toward the opponents' goal.

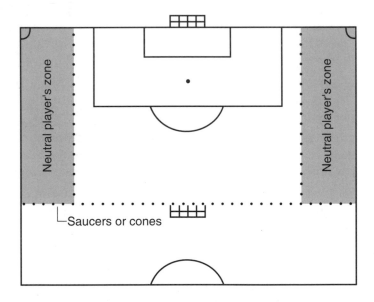

Fig. 5.5. This heading game is played under matchlike conditions on slightly less than half of a field. Neutral players on the flanks (shaded area) serve a succession of balls into the penalty area.

As the ball approaches, take a quick glance at the keeper to weigh your options before deciding what to do. Should you head the ball to the far post or just inside of the near post? Has the keeper held on the line or is she charging out to challenge for the cross? If the latter, you may choose to deflect the ball upward and over her outstretched arms. If the goalie has held on the line, you'll probably need a mixture of power and accuracy to score (the ratio of these depending on the distance separating you from the goalie at the moment that the ball is to be headed).

Most of the time you'll want to head the ball downward. Turn your body somewhat sideways to the goal to allow for more of a snapping action from the waist. As you thrust forward, contact the ball with that bone on your forehead above the eyebrow.

On crosses that sail beyond the far post you may find yourself out of shooting range. In that case, try to head the ball back across the face of the goal for a teammate to run onto.

• My favorite heading game is known as Throw-Head-Catch. As the name implies, there is a set pattern to the action. The game begins with a "kickoff" in which a player uses two hands to aim an underhand toss toward a teammate's head. The receiver must then attempt to head the ball to any teammate for that third player to catch. The catcher may take no more than two steps before throwing the ball underhand with both hands as the pattern repeats.

Opponents on the defending team may contest all headed balls as well as attempt to catch a ball after it has been headed. But no throw may be impeded.

If the ball hits the ground, the team that did not touch it last is awarded possession. Play restarts with a two-handed underhanded throw. The object of the game is to head more balls into your opponents' goal than they head into yours.

No member of the defending team is permitted inside his or her own six-yard box unless marking an attacker and/or chasing the ball after it's been played into that area. This rule prevents the defending team from packing players in front of their goalmouth in an effort to make it virtually impossible for the attacking team to score.

The field size varies depending on the number of players per side. For teams of three to five players, I suggest an area about 20 to 25 yards long and 30 yards wide. For six- to eight-player teams, the field should be extended to 40 yards long.

Throw-Head-Catch can also be played as a possession exercise. When a team achieves a predesignated consecutive number of passes, it's awarded a score. Use a large enough space for the number of players to give the attackers a chance to succeed.

© Wilfried Witters/Hamburg

Fig. 5.6. Although I often give away several inches to the forward I'm assigned to mark, my coaches are interested only in results, not excuses. Winning those 1-v-1 aerial duels is a must for defenders.

FINAL THOUGHTS

In general, South and Central American teams tend to play the ball in the air a lot less than a typical British side. But this doesn't mean that heading skills are not as important to a Mexican player as they are to an Irish player. This especially holds true in international play, where any weakness will be exploited.

As a defender I'm expected to win virtually every aerial duel I'm involved in. Strikers who can get the best of me become far more valuable to their side.

Work on your heading skills. Especially in the developmental years, these skills tend to be among the most neglected. You can consider this as a motivating factor. If you can become good in the air, you'll gain a big edge on most of your soccer peers.

Passing

"Make the ball do the work."

No matter how hard I try, I can't think of a single example of a great team that wasn't superb at passing. I'm sure you've heard your coaches imploring you to "make the ball do the work." That's because the ability to pass and move is the bread and butter of top-quality teams. And given that the ball can always move far faster than even the quickest players can run, I'm quite certain there will never be a championship team at any appreciable level of the sport that isn't adept at knocking the ball around.

To become a good user of the ball requires a combination of many skills plus tactical awareness. You will need to acquire a sophistication that allows you to consistently get into constructive supporting positions. Doing this, coupled with angling your body to achieve maximum vision, will permit you to assess all of your options before you receive the ball.

Once you've decided what to do when you've received the ball, you must be able to do it. This requires cleverness and the ability to use a wide range of body surfaces and ball flicks to disguise your intentions from defenders. You also have to be able to hit a first-touch push pass that's accurate and, as they say in coaching circles, "properly weighted" (that is, not too fast or too slow).

Like a good NFL quarterback, you should complete a high percentage of your passes, suffer few interceptions (especially on square and back passes), and be able to hit the occasional scoring bomb to a receiver sprinting behind the defense. To become a good passer you must consistently make good decisions. You'll need to recognize when to play simply and safely, and when to attempt a "killer pass." You must also learn to be discreet. As you and your teammates progress in the sport, you should be able to string passes to maintain possession until an opening is presented.

You can't be too risky. Being able to bend a 30-yard ball into a teammate's path is great, but such a pass is a weapon that even world-class players attempt only once or twice a match. Such passes, when successful, look great on the highlight films, but too often they end up on the feet of opposing players.

A combination of outstanding technical skills and tactical cleverness is almost impossible to defend. A truly great passer like former England superstar Glenn Hoddle or the USA's Claudio Reyna completes a very high percentage of their passes and can pick out a teammate far away. Claudio struck one of the greatest passes in our history in a 3-0 win over Mexico that earned the USA a berth in the 1992 Summer Olympic Games. As Claudio had the ball just beyond the midfield stripe near the right touchline, striker Steve Snow dashed down the left side of the field toward the Mexican penalty area. You might have expected the Mexican defense to push out to catch Snow offsides, but Claudio disguised his movements so well that it seemed to everyone that he didn't even know where Snow was. Looking down at the ball, Claudio pulled his right foot back ever so slightly. Before the green-shirted visitors could react, the ball was sailing over their heads. Like a shark sensing blood, Snow latched onto that 50-yard cross-field serve. His volley provided the score that put the USA in the driver's seat to stay.

Claudio's pass had everything. It was perfectly flighted, so Snow never had to break stride. It arrived deep enough in the Mexican box that Snow was well within shooting range, and yet the pass was far enough off the goal line that the keeper had no chance at an interception.

Guys who played at the University of Virginia tell me that they have trouble recalling all of the great passes they witnessed Claudio produce. As he has matured as a player, Claudio has gotten even

© Wilfried Witters/Hamburg

Fig. 6.1. Good execution requires good decision making. Even if you have the greatest variety of passing skills, without vision you'll be limited.

better at getting into positions off the ball where he's best able to slice apart a defense with a first-touch pass. If you get the chance to see him play live, spend some time studying how and when he supports. Note how well he "takes the picture" before getting the ball.

In coaching lingo, Claudio's "consideration" is superb. This means that he takes into account the strengths and weaknesses of the receiver he's passing to. A lightning-fast player is more likely to prefer the ball played into space behind the opposing defense so that he or she can run onto it. A quick but small forward playing with back to goal figures to be more successful with a ball that's laid short so that he or she can peel off of the marker. Conversely, a powerful striker will be able to hold his ground and will want the ball played right into his feet. A tall player in the opponents' penalty area will probably do better with a cross in the air than on the ground.

Some of your teammates have great skills. You can be confident that they won't panic when you play a ball to their feet, even when they are closely marked. Because of their great touch, you can strike a pass more firmly to them than you would to an average player.

On the other hand, there are those teammates whose strength isn't their touch. Even if they're open in their own third, it may not be a great idea to pass to them, as they're likely to make a hash of their first touch. All of these factors, and many more, must be considered. Your pass is only a good pass if it's the best pass you can make in a given situation. You must feel responsible for what happens to the ball after you've released it. You shouldn't feel good about your decision if the player you've just passed to has lost possession.

The receiver that Claudio picks out is almost always the one who is the most likely to do something positive at that moment. Adding to that is Claudio's accuracy. He's not content to get the ball just to an area, or even just to a player. He wants to get the ball to the *exact* spot on his teammate's foot where that player can play it both immediately and effectively.

There are several fantastic playmaking midfielders in Major League Soccer who you can learn from by observing. To really go to school on what makes these players great passers, focus on just them for long segments of a match. Keep tabs on just how many of their passes are simple, as well as how and where they run after they have played the ball.

The best playmakers are almost impossible to defend because of their ability to make their teammates more dangerous. Being able to do this with a single touch renders the effective marking of a midfield maestro virtually impossible. We were faced with just such a challenge in our upset of Colombia in the 1994 World Cup.

Carlos Valderrama was the heart of the Columbian team—*everything* went through him. One of the keys to his effectiveness was his passing accuracy; virtually every pass went just where he wanted it to go. Fortunately, we were able to choke off the middle of the field to narrow his passing lanes and assure that the teammate he got the ball to wouldn't be left running free. Nevertheless, facing a playmaker of his caliber is guaranteed to present considerable problems.

Your sharpness on game day is predicated on your sharpness on the training ground. Former NASL all-star midfielder Ray Hudson once told me about something that happened to him as a young pro that stressed to him the importance of taking pride in every pass. It was during one of his first practices at Newcastle United, and the team was engaged in a very basic drill with two slightly staggered lines facing each other. The front player was to pass on the first touch to his counterpart on the opposite line. After passing, the player was to run to the back of the other line.

This went on for a short while. Ray thought the exercise was just a casual warm-up, and he treated it accordingly. His first few passes were fine, but the next one arrived about one yard in front of his intended target. The coach then stopped the action. He walked over to Ray and commenced to verbally tear him to shreds, informing him that the playing of such a ball could easily land the receiver on the wrong end of a tackle and maybe even cost his team a match. The message was delivered without a hint of subtlety. "He just shattered me," Ray recalls.

But Ray got the point. From then on, whenever he was on a field he made every attempt to be exact with every ball he played. Credit his attitude as much as his skills for having produced the third most assists in NASL history.

TECHNICAL KEYS OF THE PUSH PASS

Because the push pass involves using a wide surface to pass the ball over short to medium distances, there's no good reason not to be consistently accurate with this pass. Toward that end, here are some of the essential technical keys:

1. When playing a first-touch push pass, always move to the ball at speed.

2. Be light on your feet so that you can adjust if the incoming ball changes its path unexpectedly.

3. Place your supporting foot next to the ball with your toes pointed in the direction at which you're aiming.

4. Strike through the center of the ball.

5. Lock the ankle of your striking foot with your toes pointed slightly upward (you toes should be a few inches farther from the ground than is your heel).

© Steve Slade

Fig. 6.2. The push pass, the bread and butter of any attacker's arsenal, requires a locked ankle throughout. The foot should swing like a pendulum through the center of the ball.

6. Follow through without rotating your striking foot. Try pretending that you're a star with a big-money shoe contract. On your follow-through, your sponsor's logo on the inside of your boot must remain visible to the camera that's directly in front of you.

TECHNICAL KEYS OF OTHER TYPES OF PASSES

At my level of the game, all of the better playmakers are fully comfortable using almost any imaginable surface to make a pass. I encourage you to experiment with using different techniques. However, you should spend the great majority of your time practicing the passes that are used most often in games—the push pass and the instep pass. That said, here are some factors to keep in mind:

1. For long instep passes that require height, lean backward and place your supporting foot so that it's to the side but slightly behind the plane of the ball.

2. To chip a ball, drive the ball of your striking foot into the ground and do not follow through. This will impart backspin.

3. When using the outside of your foot for a short pass, lock your ankle with your toes pointed downward and inward. Strike through the outside of the ball.

4. Through balls work only when an angle is created. They are very difficult to complete when you can see the front-runner's back as that player is sprinting away from you. In that case, use the outside of your foot to perform a preparation touch in which you push the ball away from your body at about a 45-degree angle so that it goes in front of you and to the side. This will improve your margin for error.

5. With a back heel, a flick, or any other disguised pass, your effectiveness will increase the longer that you wait to reveal your movements. Looking away from your target can also help to keep defenders away from your intended receiver.

© Wilfried Witters/Hamburg

Fig. 6.3. By leaning back and using my instep, I can float a pass downfield.

TECHNICAL AND TACTICAL KEYS OF COMBINATION PLAY

I imagine that you're already familiar with several forms of two-player combinations. Foremost of these are the wall pass (also known as the give-and-go or a one-two), the double pass, takeovers, run-arounds, overlaps, and underlaps. Each of these combinations requires both the technical ability to perform the task and a tactical recognition of just when to attempt it.

1. Takeovers are done in 2-v-2 situations. Given that both the passer and receiver are tightly marked, there isn't much room for error. When you're in possession, it's important that you dribble in a straight line with the foot farther from your marker while using your body as a shield. The receiver accepts the ball with the same foot as you used (left foot to left foot or right foot to right foot).

The ball is left for the player taking over and is never passed into his or her path. The player taking over should know what options exist before receiving the ball, as the first touch may present the opportunity to play a penetrating pass or to shoot.

2. The angle for a wall pass may be created either by the off-the-ball movements of the player who is to serve as the wall or by the athlete in possession preparing the ball. The initial pass must be sharp and aimed so that only the offensive player has a chance to reach it. It should be targeted at the receiver's foot that is farther from his marker.

In most cases, the receiver initiates the play by checking for the ball after having taken the marker away. The check begins with slight upper body contact to separate from the marker. As the receiver moves to accept the pass, he should glance over a shoulder to ascertain whether or not there's enough space to turn (since whenever possible the first priority is to go to goal).

Assuming that the receiver is well covered, after the playing of the first pass, the passer begins a slightly bent run behind his defender. This takes advantage of the tendency of defenders to turn their heads to follow the track of the ball.

It's the receiver's duty to play the ball into space for the teammate to run onto. That teammate must take care to accept the return pass with maximum softness so that the ball doesn't run away. The "weight" of all of the passes is vital. Strike the ball firmly but not so hard that it can't be controlled.

3. Overlapping and diagonal runs can open up a defense. It's up to the player with the ball to attack a central space by dribbling forward on a diagonal. If the first option of going to goal is unavailable, the second choice is to find a teammate who is open in the box so that he can go to goal. Alternatively, you can combine with that central player (such as when your striker shows for a wall pass). The third-best scenario is to play the ball for the overlapping teammate or one who is making a diagonal run away from the goal.

To make an overlap work best requires that you have attacked a central space. Instead of angling the ball toward the touchline, play the ball straight ahead, which will allow your teammate to receive it while running to goal.

Had you incorrectly dribbled straight ahead with your shoulders parallel to the opponents' goal line, you wouldn't be able to take advantage of the options that open up in their penalty area. In addition, a ball played for the overlapping teammate would have to be directed toward the touchline, which slows down the move by forcing the receiver to accept a pass while running away from the goal.

When a teammate in advance of the ball makes a diagonal run toward the near-side touchline, the ball is played into his or her path. Very often, this means passing the ball to the outside of the defender marking you.

4. Delivering an accurate and driven cross pass ranks among the sport's most difficult tasks. Whenever possible, use a preparation touch before hitting your cross. Cut the ball inward at about a 45-degree angle to allow for easier striking. A high percentage of attempts sail harmlessly wide of the near post because the crosser's next-to-last touch pushed the ball straight ahead toward the goal line. If defensive pressure makes the luxury of a preparation touch impossible, shorten the motion of your kicking leg so that you can strike the ball while it's still near your supporting foot. Either way, point that supporting foot at your target and strike through the middle of the ball just below its equator.

The most demanding crossing drill I've encountered had us dribbling slalom-style through a series of corner flags inside a touchline. The last flag was stationed so that our final touch was away from goal. Moreover, we had to deliver the cross quickly after clearing that final obstacle. All of this had to be done while carrying weighted poles to improve our balance. We were expected to deliver an accurate ball either by whipping in a serve to the near post or clearing the defenders and goalkeeper with a pass to a teammate unmarked beyond the far post.

5. With rare exception, aim your cross behind the line of the defense (but out of the keeper's range). Driven balls behind defenders are their worst nightmare. The attacker will be in a great scoring position if he or she gets to the ball first. Even if the defender gets there first, there's a great danger of an own goal.

The art of crossing does not come naturally to young players. But crosses are an essential part of your offensive arsenal, especially if you're a winger, a wing midfielder, or an outside defender with the freedom to overlap. Since you don't know how a coach may opt to use your skills on any future teams you play for, I definitely recommend becoming a competent crosser.

TRAINING ON YOUR OWN

Okay, it's just you and your friend the wall again. What to do? Start by practicing straight-on. Treat the ball like a yo-yo, passing it firmly with the same foot so that it comes back to the exact spot from which it was struck. This can be done on either the first or the second touch. Make sure to also work your nondominant foot.

The next step is to practice passing balls from angles while alternating feet. Challenge yourself by picking a small target and hitting it as many times as you can.

As you practice, try intentionally mis-hitting alternating strikes off the wall so that you must subsequently pass an awkward ball on the first touch. For maximum benefit, make the exercise gamelike by coming to meet the ball. Hit passes with different amounts of pace.

With all of these variations, work on the same surface extensively at one time, but be sure to work on different surfaces on different days. To be a truly first-rate passer, you must get to a comfort level with the insides, outsides, and insteps of both your feet. To maximize your rate of improvement, always be thinking of new ways to challenge yourself.

TRAINING WITH A FRIEND

Another basic exercise sees you and a friend (this time of the human variety) passing back and forth. Once again, strive for maximum accuracy by aiming for a specific foot. Make a run after each pass so that you become accustomed to passing accurately on the move.

This exercise can be adapted so that your post-pass movement is to take one step toward your partner. Soon, you'll be within a few yards of each other. At this point, exchange a few passes before taking a step backward after each pass until you're 20 to 30 yards apart. Then repeat the pattern.

Work on patterns of services. For example, use only your right foot or only your left. Or play the ball straight back and forth by using your right foot and your partner's left (or vice versa).

a

b

© Dan Herbst

c

© Dan Herbst

Fig. 6.4. Using a wall, pass the ball on the outside of the cones (a), move sideways (b), and receive it on the opposite side (c). Challenge yourself to see how many consecutive first-touch passes you can strike.

© Steve Slade

Fig. 6.5. The server at top has played the ball to the right foot of the active player, who strikes a first-touch return pass to the opposite server. That second server will then lob the ball to the active player's left foot for him to volley to the original server.

You'll discover that as you and your partner get closer to each other, the demands for accuracy and speed control are far greater. This will force you to be on your toes and to concentrate. When you're farther apart, even though the demands are not so great, don't allow yourself to get sloppy. Stay focused. It's far better to do just a few sets to maximum standards than to train for hours without incorporating the sharpness that a top-class match demands of you. Never remain stationary after any strike of the ball. In my sleep I can hear Steve Sampson reiterating, "pass and move, pass and move." Steve's right—you'd never just stand there in a game, so why do it during practice?

Here's a passing game to play with a friend. Use corner flags (or saucers, cones, bibs, or shirts) to form a goal about three feet wide. Put down saucers or use existing lines to stipulate a minimum distance from opposite sides of the goal at which each player must be stationed.

*P*ass and move.
　　　　　　—*Steve Sampson*

You can play this game cooperatively or competitively. To play cooperatively, see how many consecutive passes you can strike to your partner through the goal. You can add conditions such as passing on the first touch, passing only with your weaker foot, using only the outside of your stronger or your weaker foot to pass, or requiring that every other pass be with the nondominant foot. Try varying distances and altering the types of passes to include balls that are bent, chipped, driven, and stroked.

To play competitively, slightly widen the goal and see who can get more goals in a set time. Or you can play until someone scores 21. For variations, first-touch passes and/or those with the weaker foot or the outside of either foot could count double. Or you can play the game a la Soccer-Tennis by awarding a point to the opponent of the player who fails to successfully return the ball.

Both the cooperative and competitive versions can be played against a barrier with chalk, corner flags, or saucers marking the target area. The point begins with one player serving. The ball must strike the wall between the flags (and not higher than their tops).

© Steve Slade

Fig. 6.6. To really challenge your skills, reduce the size of the goal. You can also play this game using only the outsides of your feet.

PASSING TACTICS DRILL

With rare exception, the attacker in possession ought to have support to the left, the right, and a penetrating option to a teammate in an advanced position. Here's a drill that can help you ingrain these principles in your mind so they become instinctive. With three teammates and a ball, place a supporter nearby to either side and one in a deep-lying position (figure 6.7a).

If you (X_1) pass the ball to player X_2, as shown in figure 6.7b, X_4 moves into immediate support while X_3 drops into a deep position (figure 6.7c). Note that after the pass, you (X_1) should employ a bending run to move toward X_2 with your body in an open position. Be sure to glance over your shoulder farthest from the ball to see what's happening all over the field.

Had you (X_1) played through to X_4, as shown in figure 6.7d, then X_2 and X_3 would move toward X_4 while you stayed deep. At all times, the basic shape (one left, one right, and one deep) should be retained.

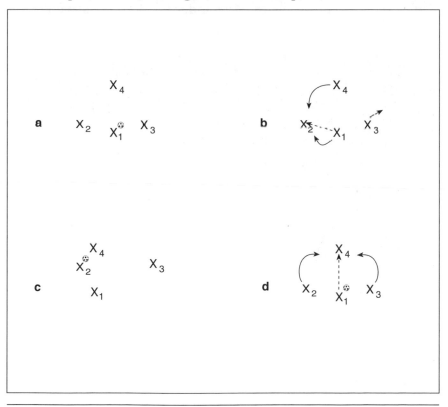

Fig. 6.7. Passing tactics drill.

PASSING GAMES INVOLVING GRIDS

After spending a few minutes doing the Practice Tactics Drill, try this exercise, which involves eight players in two adjacent grids about 20 to 25 yards square. In one grid are four attackers (who we'll call the red team) and two defenders (the blue team). Two inactive blues are in the nonactive grid.

The four reds attempt to maintain possession for as long as possible. Should a blue intercept, the ball is passed into the other grid to either of the other two blues. The two blues who won the ball then sprint to join their teammates in the opposite grid while the two nearest reds switch grids to defend. Now it's the blues who attempt to keep possession with a 4-v-2 edge.

To add more competition to the drill, try awarding a "goal" for a set number of consecutive passes and for any penetrating ball that splits the defenders. Play to a set number of goals.

You'll find that in a small-sided training exercise, the use of grids helps to demand precision. Playing under the pressure of a defender

Fig. 6.8. Playing 2-v-1 in a tight space will hone your first touch and polish your passing skills. After playing the ball, the attacker on the left should immediately make a run to his left to be available for a return pass.

in a limited space places match-realistic demands on your passing. There are several other great grid games that you can play:

- In a square that ranges from 8-by-8 to 12-by-12 yards (the more skillful you and your friends are, the less space you'll use), play 2-v-1 for possession. See how many passes you can string (with a takeover counting as a pass). The very nature of this activity demands that you pass and move. It requires you to make good decisions and execute a sharp first touch.
- A helpful progression involves three attackers and one defender. Mark the corners of a grid ranging from 10-by-10 to 12-by-12 yards. It's the defender's job to try to intercept the ball as often as possible in a 30-, 45-, or 60-second period. After each interception, the ball is quickly returned to the attackers.

There are two basic ways of playing, both of which involve seeing how many consecutive passes you can complete. One method is to

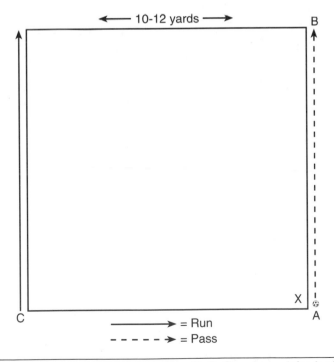

Fig. 6.9. Passing game with three attackers (A, B, C) and one defender (X). In this game, passes are directed only to an adjacent corner of the grid.

place no restrictions at all on the offensive players. An option is to require that passes be directed at one of the grid's corners, either to the immediate right or left of the passer. This option demands off-the-ball running. As shown in figure 6.9, if Player A passes the ball to B, then C must make a run to give B two options (X is the defender). Third-player movement occurs with every pass so that the athlete in possession always has immediate support in either direction.

During this drill, always open your body when in a supporting position. Figure 6.10 illustrates this principle. Note how being square to the ball (indicated by the solid line of supporting Player A) limits both your vision and your ability to change the point of attack on the first touch. The dotted line of Player B indicates how your torso should be angled.

You'll find that this exercise is far more difficult than it sounds. Try to become proficient enough that you can accomplish more than just consistently getting the ball to a teammate. Strive to become suffi-

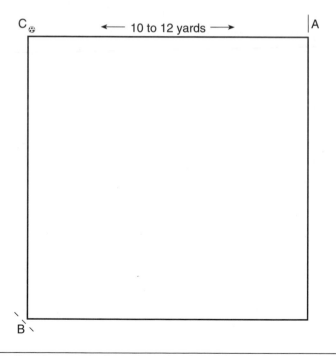

Fig. 6.10. Opening your body, as shown by player B, adds vision and makes it easier for you to deliver a pass to either attacker on your first touch. In contrast, player A is square to the ball and thus isn't aware of all his or her options.

ciently sound to be able to deliver your passes to the foot of your teammate that best allows him or her to do something constructive on the first touch. In most cases, aim for the far foot. If you can gain a good degree of "consideration" in training, you should be able to duplicate it during the pressure of a match.

• Add players and increase the space while aiming to maintain possession in a grid. You can also introduce a neutral player (or players), if you wish. Those offensive-only players can be positioned inside of or along the boundary lines of the grid.

As you improve, enforce tougher restrictions on your touches. Try awarding the defending team possession whenever a member of the offensive team touches the ball more consecutive times than is permitted.

• You can play possession grid games with three teams. In this game, known as the Three-Color Game, there are two sides on offense and a defending team that tries to win the ball back. The attackers strive to reach a set number of consecutive passes. For each pass beyond that amount, each of the defenders must do a push-up after their team finally regains the ball.

Whenever a turnover occurs, the members of the squad whose teammate lost the ball move to defense. For example, if the reds and blues are attacking with the whites defending, and a blue player has his pass intercepted, the blues are now "in," with the whites and the reds on the offensive. Such frequent changes of possession will teach you to react more quickly in transition.

A fairly substantial space is needed for this game. Except with college-level or highly advanced scholastic athletes, it's best to limit each side to five players. Since this is a vigorous activity, it shouldn't last longer than 10 minutes without a break.

• The Three-Color Game can be played with three regulation-sized goals, with each team defending one. If the blues and the whites are on offense, they attack the goal being guarded by the reds. Clever defenders may opt to pack in the area near their goal. To prevent this, award a goal to the offensive teams for completing a set number of consecutive passes (usually 10).

Following each goal, the teams that scored keep possession; the goalie who is the teammate of the scorer restarts the action by rolling out another ball. It's a good idea to maintain an extra supply of balls inside each net so you don't have to interrupt play to chase after balls kicked out of bounds.

• Knockoff is a game involving two teams and five balls placed on five saucers or T-shirts on a square grid from 20 to 25 yards wide (see figure 6.11). The objective is to use a pass to dislodge any of the five object balls off its base. Once this occurs, both the original ball and the new ball are in play until there are five live balls and only one object ball remaining. The first team to accumulate three scores is the winner. As you become more advanced, add the stipulation that only first-touch passes are permitted to knock a ball off its base.

• The Inside-Outside Game involves either 12, 14, or 16 players in and around a large circle that is divided in half by a midline. There are four zones: outside the left half of the circle, inside the left half of the circle, inside the right half of the circle, and outside the right half of the circle (see figure 6.12). In each zone, two attackers play against one defender.

Team X has the advantage inside the left half of the circle and outside the right half of the circle; Team O has the advantage inside the right half of the circle and outside the left half of the circle. Cones mark the boundaries (any ball leaving play results in a throw-in).

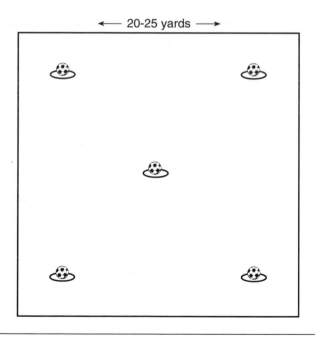

← 20-25 yards →

Fig. 6.11. Knockoff. Each circle represents either a saucer or a T-shirt on top of which a ball is placed.

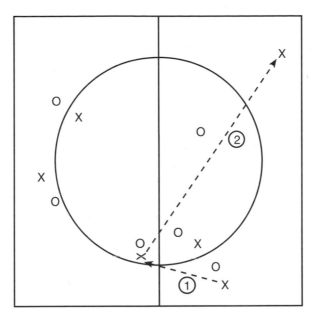

Fig. 6.12. The inside-outside game. Team X will earn a point as soon as pass #1 is played. The receiver's best option will be to attempt to split the O team members in the right half of the circle with a first-touch pass (#2) to the teammate in the upper right-hand corner. Cones may be used to mark off boundaries.

The idea is to play a pass through your opponent's half of the circle to a teammate on the other side. There are no restrictions as to what passes may be played (a ball can go from the outside of one half to the outside of the other), but a point is only awarded for a pass that goes from the inside to the outside or vice versa. First-touch penetrating balls or a scoring pass that follows a takeover can be counted as double value.

Your support position while on the inside of the circle (behind the ball, to the other side, and with your body open) is key. So too is defenders forcing the ball so as not to have to run themselves ragged.

If you have extra people, either or both of the outside zones can have three attackers challenged by two defenders (so that 14 or 16 players can participate).

One of the main benefits of this game is that it creates a matchlike atmosphere in which vision, communication, a good first touch, and the playing of penetrating balls are rewarded.

• Four-goal soccer is great for learning the principles of changing the point of attack to maintain possession while setting up a better opportunity to penetrate your opponent's defense.

Each team must defend two goals. A 25-by-25 yard area is recommended for games with four to six players per team. For more players, you'll need more space. The width of the goals can vary; 10-by-10 feet is a good starting point. The most common varieties are to place two goals on each goal line (one near each of the corner flags) or to place them centrally a few yards inside each goal line and the touchlines (see figure 6.13). With the latter, you may wish to add the stipulation that the ball must be passed through the goal to a teammate on the other side (either from front to back or vice versa). If this rule is used, increase the field size with the goals positioned about 5 to 10 yards inside the nearest boundary line.

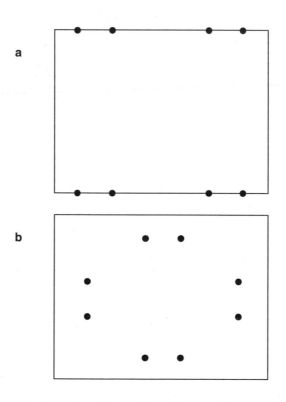

Fig. 6.13. Placement of goals for four-goal soccer: Two goals on each goal line (a), or goals placed centrally inside each goal line and the touchlines (b).

With the former, a team attacks the two goals on the opponent's goal line. A goal is awarded by passing the ball through either of those goals. With the latter, each team attacks an endline and touchline goal while defending the other two. A goal is awarded for any ball passed through one of the two goals that your side is attacking. For more advanced players, a goal counts only when the ball is then received by a teammate on the other side of the goal (thus allowing a ball to be passed either from the front of the goal to the back or vice versa). This version of the game lends itself to accommodating more players (while making the playing space proportionately more generous).

• Another favorite for players of all ages is one that Sigi Schmid used with us at UCLA. Known as the Gates Game, it has two teams competing in a large area (about 40-by-40 yards for 5-or 6-player sides—adjust this space for more or fewer players and according to player age and ability). There are several "gates," which can be formed with cones, corner flags, saucers, or shirts. Include a few more gates than there are players per team (a 5-a-side match would feature 7 or 8 gates).

A goal is scored whenever the ball is passed through any of the gates in either direction to a teammate on the opposite side. This is an activity that demands a wide range of skills; it is also economical, as it upgrades fitness while requiring players to make match-realistic decisions.

The Gates Game encourages the playing of a long ball followed by a first- or second-touch scoring pass. Thus, it closely replicates how high-level teams change the point of the attack. It also requires that players off the ball initiate penetrating runs.

As with all passing games, you can vary the activity by placing restrictions on the number of touches. Or a neutral player (or players) who is always aligned with the attackers may be introduced. You can play with unlimited touches but hold the neutral player(s) to one touch.

If you want to work on combination play, try stipulating that a goal may only be awarded after the execution of, for example, a wall pass, double pass, takeover, overlap, run-around, or underlap. Or you can play without restrictions, with the understanding that any score following a two-player combination counts double.

• You can play small-sided games with full-sized goals in which a condition is added. Foremost among these is to limit the touches of the players, as previously described.

Try altering the field's dimensions to practice a specific tactical demand. Let's say that you're engaged in 4-v-4 (plus keepers).

Making the surface long and narrow (40-by-15 yards) makes it very difficult to keep possession. The demand is to get the ball forward quickly and for withdrawn attackers to quickly move upfield to support the striker.

Making the field wide but short (20-by-50 yards) and adding a condition that all goals must be headed in will improve your possession skills (especially changing the point of attack) as well as provide ample crossing and heading opportunities. You can also do this with wide neutral players.

Playing 4-v-4 but without keepers will encourage quick shot-taking and will force defenders to close down attackers as soon as possible.

You can also play 4-v-4 plus four. Here, two teams compete in the penalty area with a full-sized goal on each endline. A third team surrounds the surface, its members acting as neutrals who are always aligned with the team that has the ball.

You can position the neutrals so that each one is about three to five yards wide of a goalpost or so that each is along one of the boundary lines. Either way, each neutral player has but one touch and may not pass to another neutral player.

As soon as a team scores, the side that conceded the goal switches places with the neutral players (but the two goalkeepers remain on).

This game can be played without keepers with a team required to string a set number of passes (or meet a stipulation such as having to execute a specific two-player combination). Once the stipulation has been met, that team may score on either goal. To add difficulty, you can require that the ball must cross the goal line in the air for the score to count or that all shots must be taken on the first touch.

• The ultimate small-sided passing game is 5-v-2, described in chapter 2. By varying the space and the limit (if any) on the number of touches, this game can be just as applicable and constructive for 11-year-olds as for our World Cup squad.

When on the outside of the circle, it's important that you provide support when near the ball and that you open your body to maximize your pre-reception vision. When taking two or more touches, make sure that your first touch changes the angle of the ball so that it rolls away from the nearer defender.

If you're supporting the ball while the defenders are wide apart, it's best to be on a plane between them. This provides you with the opportunity to split them with your first-touch pass. Attackers on the far side of the circle must read the gaps between the defenders to be positioned in a place that a split ball can be played directly to them.

As always, all of your passes should make the receiver's task simple. This game can be modified for two squads of eight players apiece. Each team has six attackers in its circle. The remaining two of its members work as defenders in the other team's circle. All rounds of the game are played for 60 seconds, with the side that strings the most consecutive passes declared the winner (a through ball counts as two passes). When time expires, the action continues until the ball is either intercepted by a defender or exits the playing area.

A PITCH FOR SOCCER-BASEBALL

Having earlier covered Soccer-Tennis and Soccer-Golf (see chapter 2), it would be almost un-American to neglect Soccer-Baseball. This game is a hybrid of soccer, kickball, and that three-strikes-and-yer-out sport. It's long been a favorite fun-filled diversion at soccer camps.

The pitcher push passes a ball for the batter to boot on the first touch into fair territory. Any kick landing in foul ground is an out. The hitter must round all of the bases and touch home before the defending team can kick the ball into an unmanned goal placed just behind home plate. All members of the batting team remain in the dugout (or at least out of the way) until it's their turn to hit.

With older players, the team in the field must kick the ball into the goal on the fly. You're limited to no more than three combined touches with no player permitted consecutive touches. If you wish to add more spice to the affair, let the batting team use a goalkeeper. How many innings you play is up to you.

Although Soccer-Baseball isn't quite the skill-builder that some of the other activities in this chapter are, the game is a lot of fun to play on occasion.

BASIC PRINCIPLES OF TEAM DEFENSE

All versions of 5-v-2 require that you apply the basic principles of defense when you're in the middle. When you're the "first defender" (the one nearer the attacker with the ball), put pressure on the attacker. Get within two feet of that opponent, angling your approach to force her to pass the ball in a specific direction. The "second defender" covers behind you to prevent a penetrating (split) pass. That defender is to the side of the ball closer to where the pass is expected to be forced.

As a pass is made, the roles of the defenders flip-flop—the second defender becomes the first defender. By making a bending run at the far side of the receiver, the new first defender hopes that the ball can be forced back in the direction of her defensive mate (who has dropped into a covering position to prevent a through ball).

It is essential that the two defenders work in sync so that their movements are coordinated and well-timed. The pressure and forcing action of the first defender only works if the second defender has already been in position to prevent a first-touch split. And as soon as the ball movement is stopped, the second defender must race to the player in possession to challenge for the ball.

*A*ll passes should make the receiver's task as simple as possible.

It's not always necessary that you gain possession via a tackle. By working together effectively you can minimize the time and space available to the attackers. Doing this will increase your chances of forcing a turnover.

Communication is important. The second defender has a greater range of vision and should inform the first defender of the direction in which the ball is to be forced. Shouting "force right!" indicates that the first defender should approach the offensive player at such an angle as to assure that the pass must be made toward the defensive unit's right side.

As the first defender, it's your responsibility to follow that command and not to get greedy. If you dive in to try to block a pass, you may have the attacker cut the ball and kick it in the opposite direction. This will strand your fellow defender in a poor position.

When you're the second defender, your top priority is to position yourself to avoid having a ball split you and your teammate. You should be about two to three times farther away from your fellow defender as she is from the opponent with the ball.

These same principles apply to all of the grid games I've described as well as to playing in a real match. Whether you're a fullback or a high-scoring striker, you should take pride in your defending. Doing so will make you a more complete player and increase your value to

Fig. 6.14. Highly respected coach Gordon Bradley says that soccer is a game of many passes and few dribbles. The more you progress in soccer, the more important becomes your ability to pass accurately and quickly and with maximum consideration.

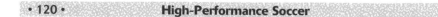

*P*lay the first ball you see.

—*Mike England*

your team. A striker who forces a foe into a bad pass in their third is often rewarded with a great scoring opportunity.

In training, your putting the attackers under great pressure will help them to improve, as it places them in a matchlike environment to test their sharpness. Only with that level of challenge can they truly progress. But remember—don't get megged!

FINAL THOUGHTS

For all of the passing games and exercises I have described in this chapter, it is important that you pay particular attention to the size of the playing area. The area must be big enough for attackers to be successful but not so large that players have too much time and space to develop bad habits.

The more you observe top-level soccer, the more you'll notice how often and quickly the ball is passed. We pros usually heed the old Liverpool motto of playing the first ball that we see (the other adage is "if you see it, give it"). The more the ball moves, the more adjusting that defenses and defenders must do. The more that they adjust, the more likely they are to expose gaps that we attackers can exploit.

Your ability in this area of the game will be more and more crucial as you advance in the sport. Take pride in developing a wide range of passing skills with all surfaces of both feet. Always strive to improve your ability to play both possession and penetrating passes.

It's been said that the mark of a truly great player is the ability to make those around him or her better. I can't second that sentiment strongly enough. Having a playmaker the caliber of Claudio Reyna in our lineup makes every one of us stronger.

However, it's also true that a team is only as solid as its weakest link. What enables our National Team to compete with the heavyweights of international soccer is that we've reached the point in our evolution where all of our members are comfortable with a ball at their feet. We can all deliver a good pass on a consistent basis.

Always challenge yourself. Whenever you play any of these passing games, you need to always be testing your skills and your ability to make quick decisions. Putting yourself under pressure from defenders in training will help you play quicker—and this, in turn, will prepare you better for the sport's demands when you graduate to the next level.

CHAPTER 7

Finishing

"To be a great scorer, you must welcome responsibility and be able to handle the consequences of failure."

One of my greatest thrills at playing in the Bundesliga was matching skills and wits with Juergen Klinsmann when he was with Bayern Munich and I played for St. Pauli.

Talk about an athlete who possesses the complete package! Juergen is technically, tactically, and physically fast. He leaps like a gazelle. He can finish with lethal effectiveness using any surface on either side. He hardly ever stops moving off the ball, and he's a master at freeing himself from his marker. His shots are almost always right on target, and they require but a half yard or a fraction of a second to launch.

Juergen's psychological make-up is first rate. When it comes to the five C's a great striker must possess, Juergen gets an A. He's composed, cunning, confident, courageous, and competitive to the max. Add it all up and you have a goal-scorer whose pedigree ranks up there among the sport's all-time greats.

Take a moment to review what I've just written, noting just how many different vital qualities I've mentioned. Subtract any of them and Klinsmann would be but a fraction of the player he has become. I tell you this in the hope that you'll realize how much more there is to goal scoring than merely becoming proficient at shooting.

It's great if you're a good striker of the ball (especially if you're equally good with both feet). While striking skill is essential to being goal-dangerous, it's but one of many required qualities. So many young players tend to judge their offensive worth by how many goals they score. But this number is not the best indication of a player's value on the offensive end.

Excelling at just a few of the attributes in Klinsmann's portfolio is generally sufficient to become a high scorer in youth or scholastic soccer (unless you're one of the fortunate handful competing at a level far above the national norm). The further you advance in the sport, the more of these attributes you'll need to maintain your strike rate.

I can't tell you how many high school hotshots I've seen who are all-everything because they netted 30 goals in an 18-game season. Yes, some of them are the real thing, but far more of them succeed because they're athletically superior to virtually all their opponents. Trust me, this type of player is considered a dime a dozen by coaches of the better college programs. You'll have a far better chance of succeeding at the next level if you score a lot less now but are competent or better at virtually all facets of being a bona fide goal-scorer.

Your first step in becoming goal-dangerous is to become technically superior. Next is to develop an awareness of situations so that you can instantaneously select the most appropriate technique to solve any specific tactical challenge.

But that's only part of the equation. You should also make an effort to become more physically imposing. Work to improve your flexibility, balance and agility, speed, upper body and leg power, and jumping skills. The best way to do this might be to solicit help from your school's or association's gymnastics coach, track coach, and weight training coach. If they see you're genuinely motivated, they'll probably be happy to show you ways to accomplish your objectives.

Once you've acquired technical and tactical skills and worked to become more imposing, faster, and stronger, you will now have the *opportunity* to become an efficient finisher. But the most important criterion, I'm convinced, is your attitude. It's often said that to be a truly great scorer requires arrogance. If you lack unbridled confidence, you will be unable to thrive in a role where most of your attempts end in failure. It takes a special type of person to remain focused on the job in spite of your marker's best attempts to distract you via an occasional well-aimed kick to the back of your legs. Moreover, like a field goal kicker, you must be prepared to hardly touch the ball for long periods of time, only to be expected to come through when the opportunity arises.

Does this require arrogance? To be sure, there's more than one contemporary striker who fits that bill. Nevertheless, I differ from the so-called conventional wisdom. Just as it's often mistakenly said that "all goalkeepers are crazy," the labeling of strikers as ultracocky creatures sounds clever but is really far from true. If anything, arrogance has led more than one player to an early demise in what is a team sport.

To be a great scorer, you must welcome responsibility and be able to handle the consequences of failure. You must believe in yourself even during the worst of slumps. But you can't be self-centered or selfish—you'll only antagonize your teammates and coaches, and without their assistance, you won't do much scoring.

It's not easy learning to walk that tightrope between the confidence you need and the arrogance you need to avoid. It's equally difficult to differentiate between the occasional (well-timed) physical payback to let that defender know that you won't be intimidated and becoming so obsessed with getting even that you sacrifice your concentration on the task at hand. Maintaining the appropriate perspective is essential for you to stay focused on putting the ball in the back of the opponents' net.

One aspect of Juergen Klinsmann that makes me marvel is how he's always thinking. Every run has a purpose. Some are to create space for his teammates by dragging markers out of position. Many are to get free to receive a pass. Others are to get on that defender's blind side to obtain the vital head start when making a run at goal in order to arrive first to a cross.

Playing against Juergen is a chess game in cleats. I can make a succession of right moves only to have the most minor of slip-ups result in a goal. Frustrating? You bet. The only consolation is knowing that I was hardly the first defender Juergen burned.

Lucky for me, I wasn't the St. Pauli player marking Juergen when he made a fantastic run in a game in which Bayern beat us 1-0 at our place (and, yes, it was Juergen who scored). It was after Juergen's goal that a Bayern player had the ball on their right flank. Juergen was at the edge of the box, about even with the far post. As his teammate prepared the ball, Juergen took two quick steps as if to

© Wilfried Witters/Hamburg

Fig. 7.1.   Not only is Klinsmann's technique flawless, just look at the determination in his expression.

begin a diagonal run toward the near post. Biting at the bait, my teammate sprinted in that direction. With Juergen behind him, he had no way of seeing that Klinsmann then took three quick steps backward. The far-post serve found you-know-who running un-marked onto the cross. Fortunately for us, his header was saved at full stretch by our keeper.

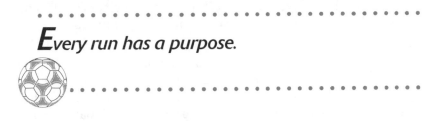

*E*very run has a purpose.

If you're a striker, spend some time studying a Klinsmann (or any of the other better front-runners in the game today) to learn how to lose your marker. Pay attention to what he does away from the ball. You'll probably notice some of the following:

1. His runs are always well-timed. Only when a teammate is free to pass *and* has made visual recognition (eye contact) will he start his sprint.

2. He runs at the goal on a diagonal—virtually never are his shoulders parallel to the goal line. Thus, during his run, he's able to see as much of the goal as possible as well as to note the positioning of the keeper. His angle of approach makes it easier to redirect balls on goal.

3. When he begins his run the ball is almost always closer to the goal line than he is.

4. For a ball that he anticipates will be played into the near post, he gets between his marker and the crosser. Before doing so, he maximizes the amount of available space in front of him by pulling his defender toward the far post. In contrast, for a serve that will be aimed in the proximity of or beyond the far post, he often takes his marker toward the crosser before running behind that defender. He understands that balls played into the near post should be driven low while far-post serves are usually lofted.

5. He knows that shots across the keeper have four chances of resulting in a goal: They can beat the goalie cleanly; they can

be finished by another attacker off a deflection; a far-post runner may produce a touch-in of a ball that's shot wide; or an own goal could be netted. In contrast, it's rare that a near-post attempt scores in any other manner than by cleanly beating the keeper.

6. He is relentless in his efforts. He follows every shot in for the rebound. He's fully aware that the great majority of goals come from shots that are taken from inside the penalty area.

7. He has an uncanny sense of anticipation that seems to always have him perfectly positioned to pounce on any loose ball in the box. There's much discussion in soccer circles about whether such a quality is instinctive or if it can be learned. I can't pretend to have any great insight to settle that debate, but I do know that when a shot is about to be taken, Juergen takes a step away from his marker toward the defender's blind side, and he usually manages to be somewhere between the far post and the point where the keeper will make the save.

8. Although I don't know his training habits first-hand, given his skills, I'm certain he must devote a great amount of time to working on his shooting. After almost every one of our National Team's practices at least a half dozen of our strikers and attacking midfielders will hit ball after ball on goal, with many of them working on swerving free kicks around an imaginary wall. Such dedication to excellence is vital to all aspects of the sport but especially in a role where there's such a fine line separating success from failure.

9. His concentration is incredible. He assumes that every ball will get to him, so he's always prepared to strike it.

10. Two cliches to which he definitely subscribes are "He who hesitates is lost" and "One hundred percent of all shots not taken don't go in." Good strikers have an itchy trigger finger. A goalie given a chance to play in the field confirms the importance of never passing up an opportunity. Invariably, they shoot every chance they get. That's because they know first-hand how little they like to face shots when they're playing in goal.

11. His selection of finishing method is one of his greatest attributes. Although he doesn't lack for power, it's rare that he strikes a ball with full force. He subscribes to one of the key

"rules" of scoring—never shoot any harder than is necessary to beat the keeper. Accuracy, not power, is responsible for most goals. And a lack of accuracy, not a lack of power, is responsible for the majority of misses. Yes, there will be times when you'll have to blast the ball. But in those cases you should concentrate on getting the ball on the framework rather than aiming for a corner. I wish I had a dollar for every rocket that sailed harmlessly over a crossbar.

The attributes of a top striker aren't far removed from those of a great matador. There are thousands of Spaniards physically capable of performing the maneuvers needed to star in the bullring. But only a special handful can perform these maneuvers when a 600-pound animal with razor-sharp horns is bearing down on them at 30 miles an hour.

- -

More goals are scored through accuracy than power.

- -

The ability to remain composed ranks among the greatest attributes any striker can possess. Much of it comes from personality. Some of it is due to an understanding of the game and to thinking ahead. When you're in or around the box, always assume that the ball will reach you. Be physically prepared and, equally important, mentally prepared to receive it. Assess the situation in advance so you know what you want to do before touching the ball.

Great strikers seem to be lucky, but I'm convinced that their ability to calculate odds accounts for their knack of being in the right place at the right time. Consider a key goal from our 3-0 win over Guatemala in round one of the 1991 CONCACAF Gold Cup.

Chris Henderson crossed a ball deep into the penalty area that was redirected by one of their defenders. Bruce Murray took a few steps toward the ball before realizing that he couldn't come close enough to it to put even moderate pressure on the Guatemalan defender who was set to head the ball away. Instead of continuing his run, Bruce retreated to the edge of the penalty area. Sure enough, the clearance came right to Bruce, who controlled it on his first touch before firing it home with his left foot.

© Jon Van Woerden

Fig. 7.2.   Once you've decided where to aim your shot, all of your focus is on the ball.

A lucky goal? Perhaps. Let's face it—nine times out of ten that defender would have hit the ball somewhere else. But Bruce's quick thinking gave him a one-in-ten chance that represented better odds than had he reacted otherwise. This helps to explain why Bruce held the record for most goals scored for the USA in full internationals (21) until Eric Wynalda bypassed him in 1996.

Because decision making is such a vital aspect of scoring, I'm not a very big fan of shooting drills. While a drill can help hone your shooting technique, scoring involves a premeditated act. Thus, the most important aspect of finishing isn't incorporated in the drill. Although I do offer some drills in this chapter to help you vary your training sessions, your emphasis should be on exercises and games that incorporate decision making.

In my opinion, the best training for scoring is to play small-sided soccer with full-sized goals guarded by keepers. Games of 3-v-3 up to 6-v-6 on fields no longer than 40 yards assure that you will confront plenty of scoring situations. Such games are far more beneficial than any drill I've come across.

But, having said that, it remains true that your shooting technique must be first-rate. Being fundamentally sound with both feet, as well as in the air, is a prerequisite to becoming an efficient finisher.

Another tip—when working on your technique, it's better to concentrate on one or two types of shooting with an emphasis on proper execution than to work for a few minutes apiece on each of several different varieties of shots. Your body will learn more through the repetition of proper execution than if you try to teach it too much at once.

Always strive to improve your skills. You should know by the feel and by that "thumping" sound of the foot striking the ball whether you've made clean contact.

Employ common sense. Shooting involves violent movements of large muscle groups. Before attempting any shots, stretch your hamstrings, your quadriceps, and if you're 13 or older, your groin. Your first few strikes should be at well below full force, gradually increasing your efforts to allow your muscle groups to adjust to the task. Unnecessarily pulling one of those large muscles is beyond foolish. A nagging hamstring injury can take a long time to heal fully.

Another demand of becoming a top-class player is self-analysis. As you well know, coaches can't call time-outs to offer suggestions. It's up to you to determine the reason that your scoring attempt was or wasn't converted into a goal.

Following a miss, try to figure out what you should do better next time. This analysis involves deciding if the nature of your breakdown was technical, tactical, and/or attributable to an absence of one or more of the five C's. If there's a discernible pattern to your misses, it's up to you to concentrate on upgrading that aspect of your finishing. Here are four of the more prevalent reasons for failing to finish:

1. You didn't identify your best option prior to receiving the ball.
2. You were physically unprepared to accept the ball.

3. You used excess power and sacrificed accuracy.

4. You rushed your attempt when there was ample time to execute a preparation touch to help open up a shooting angle.

• •

After a miss, figure out what to do better next time.

• •

TECHNICAL KEYS OF THE INSTEP DRIVE

• •

The most practiced shot involves striking the ball for power with the laces of your boot. Here are some tips for the instep drive:

1. When shooting off your dribble, prepare the ball on the next-to-last touch. If possible, use the outside of your striking foot to push the ball forward and away from your body at about a 45-degree angle. This will make it easier to get a clean strike, as your supporting foot is more likely to be next to the ball during impact. This also forces the goalie to move sideways rather than further narrowing your angle.

After preparing the ball toward the near post, it's usually better to aim your shot "behind" the keeper (that is, toward the far post). Doing so often catches the goalie still moving toward the front part of the goal with his feet not yet set. When preparing the ball toward the center of the goal, it's usually better to shoot in the same direction in which you've just moved.

Make certain that your preparation touch is long enough to allow you to run onto the ball and kick it as comfortably and naturally as possible. The preparation touch should permit you enough space to execute a natural follow-through. However, don't kick the ball so far away that an opposing defender or the goalkeeper will be able to block your shot.

Your preparation touch can kill two birds with one stone if you can beat a defender by cutting the ball back. The key ingredient is recognizing the situation.

2. The last stride with your supporting leg should be a long one. Your knee is flexed slightly, and your weight is on the front of that foot. Make certain that you're not flat-footed; the weight of your supporting leg should be on the balls of that foot.

3. Your supporting (non-kicking) foot should be pointed at your target and be next to the ball as it's struck. Planting that foot behind the plane of the ball almost always results in a shot sailing high.

4. If possible, look up before shooting to ascertain the position of the goalkeeper as well as that of nearby defenders. Once you decide where to aim, all of your focus is on the ball. Like a golfer, it's vital to keep your eye on the ball—even to the point of holding your head down after striking the ball.

5. Before hitting your shot, the knee of your kicking foot, your head, and your shoulders are all above the ball.

6. Lock the ankle of your striking foot with your toes remaining pointed downward throughout the motion. During your follow-through, the keeper should always be able to see your shoelaces—but never the cleats—of your striking foot.

7. Whenever possible, incorporate a weight shift by driving through the ball and landing on your striking foot.

8. National Soccer Coaches Association of America Director of Coaching Jeff Tipping tells his Muhlenberg College players that to shoot low they must follow through low.

9. Power derives from proper technique in which you contact the center of the ball with the sweet spot of your instep. There is no reason to swing your leg 100 miles an hour.

10. A common error on balls served from wide positions and/or shots involving a preparation touch is prematurely opening your hips. Move directly at the ball after you've prepared it or when running to meet a cross. As your supporting foot points at the goal, the rest of your body is in an open position (almost perpendicular to the intended path of the shot). When your foot moves downward to strike the ball, your hips and shoulders will automatically pivot in a counterclockwise motion (clockwise for a left-footed strike) to become square to your target. Incorporating a hip turn adds to your power without hindering your accuracy.

An early opening of the hips and shoulders may cause you to shank the shot beyond the far post. If your follow-through is across your

Fig. 7.3. As you approach the ball for the instep drive (a), your supporting foot points at your target (b), but your hips and upper body are still open (they will automatically pivot to become square on impact, thus increasing power). Your ankle remains locked throughout, with your toes pointed downward and outward. Your knee and shoulders are above the ball (c). Drive through the ball as you land on the front half of your kicking foot on your follow-through (d).

body, it's likely that you'll hit the ball with the inside of your shoe instead of with your instep. The technical correction is to make a concerted effort on subsequent shots to be sure that all of your movements between the preparation touch and the planting of your supporting foot are directed toward the spot from which you will strike the ball. In the case of a first touch shot and/or a volley, run directly toward the spot from which you anticipate your strike will occur.

TECHNICAL KEYS OF OTHER COMMON FORMS OF FINISHING

The instep drive is practiced most often by players who are working on their shooting. However, a considerable percentage of goals come from close-in thanks to the use of the inside of the foot. Don't just work on hitting 25-yard drives. The first-touch redirection of the 6-yard touch-in should not be neglected.

1. When side footing the ball with a push pass-like technique, the weight of your supporting leg should be on the balls of that foot. Make contact with the upper third of the ball so it stays low. The knee of your striking leg is flexed and over the ball prior to contact. As always, the non-kicking foot points at your target.

2. To chip a shot, place your supporting foot behind the plane of the ball. Aim toward the far post, as this allows for a longer flight and provides greater distance for your shot to dip.

3. Leaning back and away from the ball will impart swerve (right to left on a right-footed attempt and vice versa). The inside of your striking foot makes contact against the far outside of the ball, with your toes pointed slightly upward as your ankle is locked. The angle of approach is flat (a player taking a right-footed inswinger free kick will often start the approaching run from about three to five yards directly to the left of the ball). Aiming just past the far post on a shot that's to be swerved is almost always your best option to open up the goal.

Your supporting foot remains grounded throughout the motion. Some of my teammates lean their bodies so far that their weight is actually borne by the outside of the supporting foot. It's amazing that they don't roll their ankles while doing so.

a

b

© Dan Herbst

Fig. 7.4. To add swerve, lean back and away from the ball with your weight on the outside of your supporting foot (a). Strike the far outside of the ball with the inside of your boot and follow through across your body (b).

4. To reverse the curve, simply use the outside of your foot against the near side of the ball, with your supporting foot well behind the ball. Thus, your right foot would strike the ball at about nine o'clock. Your ankle is rigid, with your toes facing downward. Follow straight through the ball.

5. On a side volley, keep your body square to the flight of the incoming cross. Point your supporting foot at the target. Lower the goal-side shoulder so that your striking foot's trajectory is slightly downward to help keep the ball low. Make contact just above the center of the ball.

6. On a half-volley, try to strike the ball as close to the ground as possible. The farther the ball is from the turf, the harder it will be to keep your shot low. Make sure that the knee of your striking leg remains forward of that foot, with your toes pointed downward throughout. Follow through low. Keep your ankle locked. Remember, don't let the goalie see your cleats.

7. As with a half-volley or a side volley, the pre-shot positioning of your supporting foot is critical on a volley. Make sure that your non-kicking foot is next to where the ball will be struck (having it behind the plane of the ball makes it extremely difficult to keep your shot below the crossbar). Place the knee of your kicking foot over the ball and lock your ankle so that your toes remain pointed downward throughout the leg swing, including the follow-through.

Shifting your weight to land on your kicking foot will increase the power of your volley, but with anything less than near-perfect split-second timing it can also hurt your accuracy. Except on very long attempts, the pace of the incoming ball coupled with solid contact with the foot's sweet spot should give you ample power without shifting your weight.

8. To dip a volley, strike the ball with the front of the boot (just below the final eyelets of your shoelaces). Keep your ankle locked, don't shift your weight, and hold a low follow-through. Place your supporting foot just behind the plane of impact.

9. With any form of shooting—but of special importance with all forms of volleying—use the opposite-side arm from your striking foot for balance. That arm can also be used to gain leverage while holding off the challenge of an opponent.

10. The idea of the game is to score goals. Toe-pokes may not earn style points, but they can be deadly from close range.

© Dan Herbst

Fig. 7.5. For a side volley, lower the shoulder closer to the goal to help your leg swing downward as you contact the ball just above its center. Lock the ankle of your shooting foot. Use a short leg swing, as you'll have no problem getting power if you strike the sweet spot of the ball with the sweet spot of your foot.

11. If you aren't in possession of the ball but find yourself in a potential shooting situation, move to the ball (if you don't, someone else will).

TECHNICAL KEYS OF 1-v-1 SITUATIONS (BREAKAWAYS)

Here are some suggestions for ways to improve your chances when it's just you and the keeper:

1. As goalies are trained to advance forward on any long touches, keep the ball under control at all times.

2. Calculate when the next-to-last touch before confronting the keeper will occur. If necessary, use that touch to alter the angle of the

© Steve Slade

Fig. 7.6. To dip a volley, contact the ball with the very end of your foot (at the top of the toes).

ball to freeze the keeper so that he can't dive into your feet on the next touch. You can also freeze the keeper by faking a touch as you run at the keeper. It's your aim to get the keeper to commit first, or at least to get his weight back on his heels (which makes it virtually impossible for him to move effectively).

3. The closer you are to the goalie, the more important it is to keep the ball low and to just get the ball past the keeper. Using the outside of your foot to disguise your shot requires only a minimal leg swing, so the keeper has hardly any time to hit the ground.

4. By keeping the ball within striking distance as you run with it, you can use subtle leg movements and shoulder dips to fake a shot. It's your intention to get the goalie to commit his body *before* he is close enough to dive into your feet. As soon as the goalie's body collapses, you have several options:

- Strike the ball firmly while keeping it on the ground. The outside of your foot, with your toes pointed downward, is an efficient striking tool, but there will be situations where you have so little time that a toe-poke is required.

- If time and space permit, use the inside of your foot. Concentrate on striking the top third of the ball.

- Very often, a chip will work in this situation. Punch your foot straight into the ground. Hit the bottom of the ball just firmly enough to clear the keeper but not so hard that it clears the crossbar.

- Try rounding the keeper. This is particularly effective when the keeper's stance is excessively upright or when he's running out of control in your direction. Be aware that proper goalkeeping technique calls for advancing when the ball is not being contacted by the attacker's feet and to keep the hands low with palms facing the shooter whenever the offensive player has the ball within striking distance.

  Should you opt to dribble the goalie, keep the ball out of his range (the goalie knows that just getting a fingertip to the ball is enough to alter its path and thwart your attempt). One word of caution: The closer you get to the goal line, the less margin for error you'll have.

TRAINING ON YOUR OWN

After stretching your major muscle groups, you can begin the technical aspect of your training. My rule of thumb is start off slow and build to more powerful types of shots.

Your warm-up may involve the ongoing first-touch striking of shots off a wall with your instep. Do this with the same foot or alternating feet, varying your distance from the wall. Take pride in hitting a target to get accustomed to the feel of a clean strike with your toes down and your ankle locked.

This may also be done with a volley (which may require a second touch with the first contact used to set up your shot). Also work on hitting shots off the dribble following a preparation touch.

As you know by now, to receive maximum benefit from training you need to simulate match conditions. Move to the ball at speed, look up to pick a target before refocusing your attention on the ball, and use the appropriate amount of power for the distance you are from the imaginary keeper.

You can also serve balls to yourself. Standing about 20 to 30 yards from the wall and with your back to it, toss the ball over your head. Now pivot and shoot the ball quickly. Don't hesitate in an effort to hit the ball in the most comfortable position. Instead, react as if your time and space are as limited as they will be in a game.

Vary your tosses so you can practice hitting balls on your left, on your right, directly in front of you, on the ground, and bouncing. To add challenge, impart spin to your tosses.

Of course all of this can be done on a goal instead of a wall—the only negative is that you'll have to retrieve all of your shots. This is an inefficient use of time, which means that you'll get less strikes per minute than when working with a wall. However, there is something to be said for using the same target as in a match. There's also *a lot* to be said for having a good friend who happens to be a goalkeeper.

It's better to have a goal than a wall when you practice bending your shots, which is something I practiced a lot. Aiming for the far side-netting, I'd hit my first attempt from the 6-yard box and follow it with shots from the penalty spot, the 18-yard line, and just beyond the top of the D (the semicircle outside of the penalty area). I can also remember a goal near my home that featured a rather taut net. I'd whack a shot with full power from close range and then do the same with the rebound.

TRAINING WITH A FRIEND (OR TWO)

For your warm-up, stand about 10 yards apart. Boot the ball firmly with your instep, aiming at your friend's feet. You may kick back and forth on the first touch, or one of you may receive balls while the other one serves grounders. This can also be done with the active player backpedaling while the server jogs forward, or vice versa. At all times, striking the ball cleanly is your number one objective.

Next, punt balls back and forth. Your ankle should remain locked, with your toes pointed downward as you attempt to hit every shot into your partner's chest.

If you have a wall or a goal at your disposal, have your partner serve balls from various angles, distances, and speeds. Run onto those passes and shoot on the first touch. The combination of a moving ball and a mobile player makes it far more difficult for your supporting foot to be in the optimal position as your striking foot impacts the ball. Developing the coordination of those movements is important in being able to consistently strike a ball cleanly and accurately.

In many ways, this is basic stuff. Nevertheless, we pros practice our fundamental skills over and over again. That's because we know all too well that there's never been a perfect player. We can all improve. To continue to improve requires a lot of repetition and routine, even once you've reached a high level of skill.

Shooting drills are sometimes as mundane as lining 10 balls across the top of the penalty area and letting your foot fly. You shoot a ball, take a step back, and then shoot the ball next to it. Shoot rapid fire until you can consistently hit your target 10 consecutive times, keeping your shots low. You can also push each ball forward and to the side before shooting on the next touch.

Another exercise is to stand at the top of the D with your back to goal and your legs spread apart. The server has a ball at his or her feet that is gently passed through your legs. Pivot and race to that ball for a shot at goal. Have balls passed to either side of you.

Variations include your sitting on the ground and having a friend roll a ball. Get up as quickly as possible and run to that ball for a shot.

Work on your "family" of volleys. With your back to the goal, toss the ball over your head. Turn, take the picture of the goal and the keeper, and focus exclusively on the ball as you prepare to strike it. This, too, can be done with a server.

Another exercise is to mark off "goalposts" at regulation width (24 feet) by using corner flags, cones, saucers, or shirts. You and a friend are on opposite sides of the goal, with a keeper between you. Alternate shots from distance on either the first touch or after a preparation touch. If you want to, keep score. You can also do this exercise with one of you chipping a long ball over the keeper to the player on the opposite side. You can play this two ways—with the receiver shooting on the first touch or having the option of employing a preparation contact.

You can also do the exercise with two attackers on each side. You and your partner play the ball back and forth a few times. Then when the pass comes a few yards in front and to the side of the shooter, she must strike the ball with the first touch.

Or try the exercise with one member of each team on each side of the goal. The passer plays the ball to the receiver's feet. As soon as the ball reaches the receiver, the passer becomes an active defender. This forces the receiver either to shoot immediately or to prepare the ball away from the pressuring opponent with the first contact before shooting on the next touch.

This game can be as demanding as befits your skill level with, for example, the passer/defender chipping the ball to the receiver/ shooter.

SCORING EXERCISES

Try playing a game in which two full-sized goals guarded by keepers are approximately 40 yards apart. As figure 7.7 illustrates, Team X and Team O compete to see who can score more in a set time frame (or a set number of attempts).

Player X_2 passes diagonally to X_1 after X_1 has run forward to show for the ball. That ball is laid off for a first-touch shot on goal by X_2. X_1 and X_2 then run to the back of the opposite line. As soon as they're finished, the action then goes in the opposite direction with O_2 getting a shot at the other goalkeeper. An alternative is for the players to work a double pass so that the player who starts the move also concludes it by taking a shot.

One of my favorite childhood shooting games helped me develop confidence in taking on defenders in 1-v-1 situations in the attacking third of the field. It starts with a ball placed about 40 yards from a lone goal. The attackers (Team X in figure 7.8) are in a straight vertical line. The player at the front of that line passes to any one of the opponents (Team O). That opponent immediately returns the pass to the attacker, and a one-on-one confrontation occurs, with the offensive player striving to score. The restrictions are that the defender must play a good ball back to the attacker, and the offensive player must play direct (in a game, there isn't time to lollygag while in possession in and around the opponents' penalty area). Each member of the offensive team gets one chance before the teams trade places. Keep track of which squad scores more. A team must capture a set number of rounds to be declared the winner.

This game can also be played as a 2-v-1. Once again, there isn't any restriction on the attackers except for the stipulation that they must go to goal expeditiously.

Another 1-v-1 activity begins with both the defender and the attacker facing the goal from about 35 yards out. The defender has the ball and initiates the action by dribbling at the goal, with the

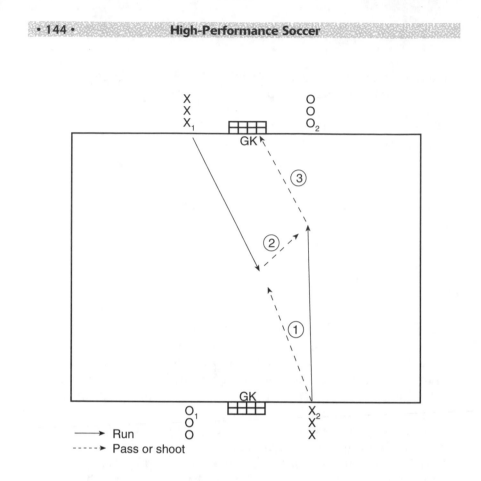

Fig. 7.7. In this exercise, the action is initiated by X_1 showing for the ball. X_2 plays a crisp pass to X_1 and immediately sprints to get in on the end of a wall pass. To test yourself, have X_1 chip the pass so that you must strike a half-volley.

attacker chasing a few yards behind. At whatever moment the first player chooses, the ball is stepped on and left for the attacker. It's now up to the offensive player to score by getting around that defender before shooting or, alternatively, firing on goal while using the marker to screen the keeper.

Figure 7.9 shows all of the seven athletes of Team O with three balls apiece. One of the O members passes the ball gently forward so it runs about three yards beyond an X (who starts with his or her back to the goal). X pivots and attempts to get off a shot before the O chases him or her down. Whenever possible, a first-touch shot incorporating a weight shift is ideal. Remember that if you're in the penalty area the toughest save for the goalie is often a hard-hit ground ball that's a foot

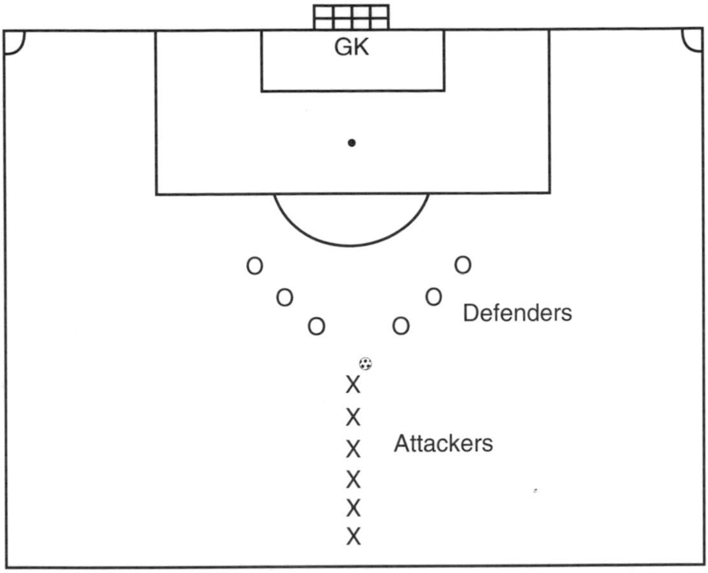

Fig. 7.8. This game was one of my childhood favorites. Place a ball about 40 yards from the goal. The player at the front of the line of attackers (Team X) passes to any member of Team O. The defender returns the pass to the attacker, and they go one-on-one as the attacker tries to score.

or so to either side of the keeper. To hone your volleying, try this with the O tossing the serve either over that X or bouncing the ball to his or her side. For this game to be of any real benefit all players must avoid cheating—which means that it's everyone's duty to provide a useful serve.

Another variation is to have the members of Team X facing the goal. The ball is served over a shooter's head. The server isn't permitted to run into a defending position until the attacker has reacted to the ball. Once again, if possible, a first-touch shot is usually preferable.

Figure 7.10 illustrates a game that involves two teams of seven players apiece (although you may vary the number) with a like number of balls, plus a goalkeeper. There are no defenders, so the nonactive team serve as ballboys while stationed behind the goal.

Each member of the shooting side gets one attempt. However, whenever a player's strike is off-target, the entire team must sprint in the same predesignated direction (either clockwise or counter-clockwise) around the goal before returning to their original positions to continue the round. The team that scores more is the winner.

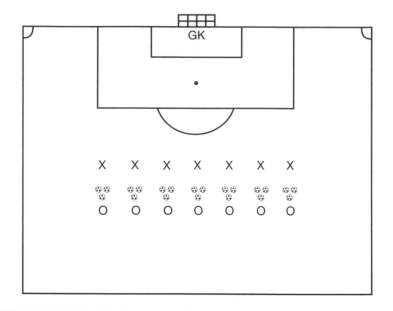

Fig. 7.9. This game will help you improve your ability to shoot quickly while on the move under an opponent's pressure. Concentrate on hitting the target so that, at the very least, you force the keeper to make a save.

Although the activities I've described so far have all included keepers, this doesn't always have to be the case. A member (or two) of the defending team can go in goal, with the stipulation that using their hands and arms is prohibited. This provides practice for clearing balls off the line.

A real favorite involves two defenders in the goal with the attackers taking turns dribbling through the cones slalom-style (see figure 7.11). Place four to six cones in diagonal lines with about two to three yards of space between them. The last cone should be at least five yards from the top of the penalty area. A preparation touch is used before the ball is struck from outside the penalty area (you can lengthen or shorten the distance to suit your needs). You'll begin to tire after your second or third shot, but make an extra attempt to drive through the ball to land on your kicking foot and to combine that power with accuracy. Retrieve your ball after shooting and dribble at speed to the back of the opposite line.

The defenders are permitted only one touch to scramble shots off the line. They may clear the ball anywhere, with the shooter forced to run down his or her own ball. All remaining members of the

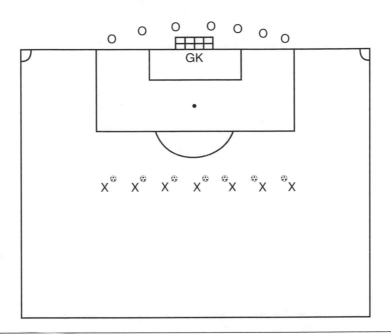

Fig. 7.10. In this game, each member of the shooting side (Team X) gets one attempt to score. Take pride in striking the ball powerfully while hitting the target.

defending team are responsible for retrieving any balls that enter the goal and immediately passing them back to the scorer.

The team netting more goals in a set time frame (usually two to three minutes) wins that round. Play enough rounds of competition to give everyone a chance to defend the goal.

A scoring system that encourages accurate shooting is to award three points for every goal scored and one point for any shot that's on target. A ball that rebounds back into play after hitting a goalpost or the crossbar, or one that would have been in the net had it not been saved, are considered to be on target. Regardless of how good a shot you strike, no points are awarded if you missed a cone while dribbling or shot after crossing the line.

It's a plus to have a lot of free space behind the goal so that inaccurate shots are punished. Once a defender has cleared a missed shot, the shooter must sprint to retrieve the ball to avoid missing a subsequent turn. Just a few such needless runs convince shooters of the value of hitting the framework. Do take care to use only hand-stitched balls and make sure they aren't overinflated.

For sheer fun, there are few soccer games you'll enjoy more than World Cup. It's an every-kid-for-himself elimination contest. The

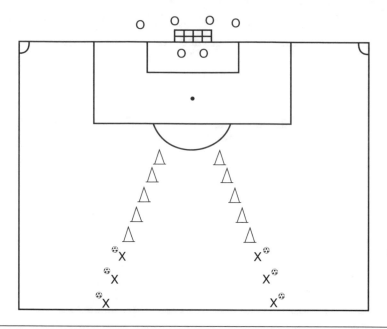

Fig. 7.11. You'll be surprised how physically demanding this game can be. As a member of Team X who has just dribbled through the cones, you'll shoot with the kind of fatigue you'll often experience in games.

server sends a ball into a crowded penalty area. All of the participants—except, of course, the goalie—attempt to score.

Goals are credited to the last attacker to touch the ball before it crosses the goal line and enters the goal. A player who scores is considered "safe" and leaves the playing area. A new ball is then served. This continues until only two attackers who have yet to score remain in the area. These two players battle until one is eliminated. Players ousted from the game serve balls during subsequent rounds.

Once the first participant has been eliminated, all the safe players return to compete until one of them is knocked out. Eventually, only two players will remain. The World Cup Final is a best two-of-three goals affair.

To keep the action moving, stipulate that a ball is dead the moment it's cleared or when a player dribbles it away from the goal. This forces you to shoot at every opportunity instead of waiting until the ball is in an optimal position.

You can also play World Cup with teams of two players apiece. And you can play it in a 20-yard long space with a goal at either end so that virtually every cross assures a scoring attempt.

THE BEST WAY IS THE REAL WAY

In my opinion, small-sided games with full-sized goals remain the best way to develop your goal-scoring skills. These games ensure many scoring chances, and each opportunity will require match-realistic decision making from the shooter.

To maximize scoring chances, add some neutral players who always play with the team that has the ball. For example, a 4-v-4 game may feature two such athletes so that the attackers always enjoy a six-on-four edge.

One danger is that players on the offensive team become too patient because of their numerical superiority. You want to develop the mentality to shoot on the first good opportunity. To emphasize that attitude, play without goalkeepers (you may wish to stipulate that for a score to count, the ball must enter the goal on the fly). Here are some other options:

• Score any first-touch shot that's on target as a goal and have any first-touch shot that goes into the goal count for three.

• Play a normal game but with the condition that a penalty kick is awarded to the defending team whenever an attacker hesitates to shoot in a situation in which a shot was warranted.

• Use a midfield line on a field that's 36 to 50 yards long. In the half of the field closer to a team's own goal, the defending team has a three-on-two edge, with all participants restricted to their own zone. The ball must be passed across the midfield line to one of the two strikers. The objective is for that forward to cut the ball back for a teammate to run onto for a first-touch, long-distance strike that finds the back of the net.

• Play on about a 40-yard long surface, as we do with the National Team, using these rules:

1. A two-touch limit is enforced when you have the ball in the same half of the field as the goal you're defending.

2. All players on the attacking team (except for their goalie) must be in the offensive zone before a shot can be attempted. This reinforces the important tactical habit of pushing up together as a team. As a defender, one of my golden rules is that I run forward whenever the ball goes forward. The concept of team movement is one that you must acquire, as it will be demanded of you at higher levels of the sport.

3. A goal counts double if any member of the defensive team isn't in his or her defending half of the field when the shot is taken.

• When you've got lots of friends, try a game of 8-v-8 (plus keepers) on a field that's about twice the length of a penalty area (roughly 36 yards long). Each team has four players on the field, with the others positioned to either side of the opponents' goal on the goal line that you're attacking. Thus, when on offense, you'll enjoy an 8-v-4 advantage.

You may pass the ball to any of your teammates, including the those on the goal line (however, these teammates are limited to a single touch).

Fig. 7.12. Romanian star Gheorghe Hagi used the inside of his foot to score on this penalty kick in the 1990 World Cup.

FINAL THOUGHTS

For reasons that I can't fathom, a lot of coaches spend less time working on finishing and its various components than they do on passing, dribbling, and receiving. Small wonder that it's so common to see a team dominate a game and yet fail to win.

There's only one meaningful payoff for superior skill. It results when your team turns all of its great tactical application of techniques into something tangible—the scoring of a goal. Your ability to feature a broad range of shooting skills when married to athleticism and the five C's will make you a most valuable player. Players who consistently put balls in the net are worth their weight in gold (and goals).

Don't neglect this tremendously important aspect of soccer. Work long and hard on your own and with friends to become a better striker of the ball. When you play small-sided games try to use a regulation-size goal protected by a goalkeeper. Adding a decision-making aspect to your drills as often as possible is essential, as making good decisions in a split-second is a prerequisite for becoming a bona fide marksman.

8

Goalkeeping

"*Always believe in
your abilities.*"

During my tenure with the National Team I've seen so many goalkeepers come and go that I feel I've become something of an expert regarding the strengths and weaknesses of that breed. As of press time, the list included Kasey Keller, Tony Meola, Brad Friedel, Juergen Sommer, Marcus Hahnemann, Zach Thornton, David Vanole, Winston DuBose, Arnie Mausser, Jim Gorsek, David Brcic, and Tim Harris. One of them is now the agent to a current teammate (but I can't speak ill of him because he's a fellow UCLA alumnus). Others who had a cup of coffee at this level during that same time period in games I didn't play in include Mark Dodd, Jeff Duback, Ian Feuer, Steve Fuchs, and Scoop Stanisic.

All of them had to be quite good to reach the National Team plateau. Almost every one of them stands better than six feet tall, is extremely athletic in his movements, and has the "soft" hands a goalie must possess. They tend to have assertive personalities. I'm convinced that the differences between the handful who had a long-term impact at the professional or international level as opposed to the "here today, gone tomorrow" types are more psychological than physical.

I will spend the next several pages reminding you of the technical keys of shot-stopping and offering some of the exercises I've seen professional goalkeepers perform. But as important as it is to build your repertoire of goalkeeping skills, a factor that's even more vital to your ultimate success as a goalie is your attitude.

Top-class goalies all feature an unmistakable aura of confidence that rubs off on their entire defense. Because they are so composed under pressure, they help their defenders to be composed. But you can never be sure how much of the cool calm you see in goalies is real and how much is an act they must perform because their teammates expect it of them. I'm reminded of an interview I once heard Steve Martin conduct in which he declared that the most important aspect of comedy was sincerity. And what do you do, he was asked, when you can't be sincere? "Then," he replied, "you have to fake it!"

I think it's much the same for being confident when playing in goal. It's essential that your teammates believe that you believe in yourself. The best bet is to be confident in your abilities. But if you have your doubts, make certain that nobody knows about them but you. One of Tony Meola's greatest assets is that he *always* projects himself positively.

Inspiring the confidence of your defensive unit is vital. The same squad will play a lot better in front of a positive goalie than one who appears negative, worried, or nervous. If I'm certain my keeper will deal with a cross, I don't feel the need to lunge to block the ball. If I have suspicions about my goalie, I may feel compelled to dive to make a stop, which could allow the opponent to cut the ball, get behind me, and unbalance our defense.

A defense that is scrambling about with little control is often a symptom of the all-too-common problem of low confidence in themselves and in their goalie. Conversely, if you can make your defenders feel at ease, you're far less likely to face as many difficult situations.

• •

Inspire the confidence of your defenders.

• •

The best keepers possess a consistency of decision making. As a defender, I know when they will come for a cross and when they'll hold on their line even before I hear their shout to clear the ball ("away!") or to step aside ("keeper!"). I know that they will have their angles right, that they'll do their part in organizing the defense, paying particular attention to directing me when I'm on the weakside, and that their distributions will be intelligent and accurate. I appreciate that they are willing to put their body on the line and make whatever personal physical sacrifice is required to keep the ball out of the net. Yes, it's great if they can pull off that dramatic full-stretch diving fingertip save to redirect a shot around the post, but as big a psychological lift as that is for a team, such a play isn't nearly as valuable as consistency. It's the ability not to yield the so-called soft goal that distinguishes the keepers who are excellent over time.

My first World Cup in 1990 was the last one for Peter Shilton. Remarkably, despite the many outstanding English goalkeepers challenging him for his shirt, he was the top choice from when Gordon Banks retired after the 1970 World Cup until a generation later. The international career in which he earned a remarkable 125 caps spanned from Pele to Diego Maradona. Shilton's debut in a 3-1 win over East Germany at Wembley Stadium came 16 days before Chris Henderson, the youngest member of our 1990 World Cup squad, was born! Long after we were eliminated, there was Shilton leading

England into the semifinals, yielding but three goals in his five matches up to that point.

Likewise, the previous two World Cups had featured "senior citizen" goalkeepers who, though past their 40th birthdays, were still at the top of their game. In 1986 Pat Jennings started every match for Northern Ireland. Four years earlier Dino Zoff had captained Italy to World Cup glory. His remarkable full-extension dive only moments before injury time deprived Brazil's Oscar of what appeared to be a certain equalizer. That save, which remains one of the greatest and most dramatic in World Cup history, allowed his nation to hold on to a 3-2 result that assured their team's passage into the semifinal round. Zoff then shut out Poland in the semis and held the West Germans scoreless in the Final until yielding a meaningless 84th-minute Paul Breitner strike. By that time the Italians had already put three of their own shots past losing goalie Harald Schumacher.

What kept Shilton, Jennings, and Zoff around so long was their consistency. Shilton, in particular, rarely had to make an eye-catching save, precisely because his positioning and anticipation were so remarkable. I can honestly say that I don't ever recall seeing him make a hash of handling a cross.

Aside from being fundamentally sound and psychologically stable, such consistency is a result of how one approaches the sport. Almost every great goalkeeper is equally as solid in practice as in a game. They don't believe that they can turn on and off like a light switch. Their attitude is that any score against them is a personal affront. Their desire to maintain a "clean sheet" is nearly as strong on the training ground on Tuesday morning as it is in the stadium on Saturday afternoon.

The importance of proper training habits can't be overemphasized. With very rare exception, goalkeepers are tested a lot more in practice than in a game (you will probably make more saves in a half hour of practice than in a month's worth of matches). As a keeper, if you're lazy or lack adequate concentration during training, you'll squander your best opportunity to improve. And you'll lose the respect of your harder-working teammates as their confidence in you diminishes with every shot you fail to stop.

Another important aspect to having the right attitude is to remain on an even keel after yielding a goal, even if it comes in front of 50,000 witnesses and it was your fault. Even world-class keepers occasionally make costly blunders, and you will, too. Once that ball gets past you there's absolutely nothing you can do or say to remove that digit from the scoreboard. Giving up goals comes with the territory, so don't lie on the ground like some sort of beached whale and bemoan your fate. The sight of a goalie pounding his fists into the turf only deflates the team while lifting the opposition.

You can't let an error affect your attitude, especially as a goalie. The object of the game isn't to avoid mistakes. Playing that way will only make you tentative. If making no errors was an honor, we'd all strive to be substitutes—because on the bench, we are free from fault! So, even after a mistake, retain a positive attitude. Don't scream at your defenders for having the audacity to be imperfect. There's no use acting like a jerk when a teammate fails to perform up to your expectations. After all, if we never made mistakes, you goalies wouldn't have a job!

Fig. 8.1. Of all of his outstanding attributes, Tony Meola's greatest quality may be how he exudes confidence.

There's a tale about the second-division defender who gets beaten by a striker, who then proceeds to score. This happens a second and then a third time. The exasperated keeper shouts, "If you ever learned to mark a man, you'd be in the first division." To which the defender replies, "Yeah, and if you'd made that save, we'd both be in the first division!" The moral: Don't point fingers.

One of the most difficult challenges for a goalkeeper is to maintain concentration when the action is at the other end of the park for what seems like forever. It's easy to become unfocused, fall out of rhythm, and lose the mental sharpness you need. Such lapses in action at your end can be more damaging than facing continuous pressure, as pressure keeps you alert.

One trick to help keep your mind on the match when your team has continuous run of play is to yell occasional instructions to your teammates. A lot of keepers will also hop around a bit or run a few yards to stay loose.

When watching a professional match, notice that virtually every team pushes its defenders up to the midfield line when the ball is in the attacking third. As a goalkeeper, you're responsible for covering the space between yourself and your last defender. By standing at or beyond the top of your own penalty area, you're better positioned to deal with any balls played over the top. Moreover, you're closer to the game, which should help you maintain concentration.

The way that you communicate with your teammates is every bit as important as what you tell them. The tone of your voice must convey urgency without a trace of panic. Offer all needed direction, but don't engage in a nonstop monologue. Keepers who incessantly babble are eventually tuned out by their teammates. Like the boy who cried wolf, when they finally do say something important, it's unlikely to be heeded.

Given the back pass law, the modern goalie is a lot more than just a shot-stopper. Today's keepers must be competent at receiving an awkward ball with either foot (and with all other soccer-related body parts). They should also be able to pass accurately with either foot. Really, they need most of the skills all other soccer players require. Acquiring these techniques doesn't happen by accident. It's not uncommon for today's professional keepers to take part in our five-a-side training games or to join us when we play 5-v-2. While you wouldn't confuse Kasey and Brad with Claudio Reyna, they're both solid in the field. In fact, Tony Meola scored 33 goals while playing up front during his senior year at Kearny High School in New Jersey.

I've heard many coaches declare that it's even more important today that their goalies be a part of the team and not be apart from the team. Yes, there are occasions when our keepers do run down to the far end of the training facility to practice on their own with their specialized trainer, but they are also integrated into the majority of most sessions. This is important for honing their field skills and for the bonding between players that helps create a positive team chemistry.

As a goalkeeper, your physical stature becomes more significant as you progress to higher levels of soccer. Many experts feel that the transition from youth/scholastic play to the college game is more difficult for keepers than for any other position. Shots on goal are harder and more accurate. Physical challenges for crosses come from bigger and stronger opponents who jump higher.

According to ex-pro player and SoccerPlus Goalkeeper School Assistant Director Bernie Watt, "Most high school goalies are shot blockers. They tend to be really good athletes who keep the ball out of the net. But many of them don't catch extremely well, and their ability to organize and direct their teammates needs to be greatly improved." So, too, he says with their handling of crosses that "now will be driven instead of floated. And the faster speed of play requires a faster speed of thought by the goalie."

Your handling is a major concern. Avoid taking the easy way out in practice. Whenever possible, attempt to hold every shot and cross. In a game, the rule is "safety first." But in training it's okay to make positive mistakes that will help you improve. Don't be content to parry away the ball in a challenging situation.

Use old gloves or, better yet, no gloves at all. If you can improve your technique to be able to hold shots without the aid of equipment, you'll fare even better in a match when assisted by a good pair of gloves.

Another concern, according to Bernie, is that most youngsters aren't physically prepared for college and/or professional soccer. Readying yourself to compete at the next level requires upgrading your strength and the explosiveness of your legs.

Recommended exercises for leg power include jumping rope, two-footed jumping over a ball with your knees high (both side-to-side and back-to-front), one-footed hopping to touch the crossbar, and practicing your diving on sand. Your upper body work should incorporate chin-ups, push-ups, and weight training with an emphasis on repetitions instead of on heavier weights. Consult a qualified instructor who can help to design a program that best meets your specific needs.

TECHNICAL KEYS OF GOALKEEPING
• •

Not many staffs of youth or high school teams include a coach who is well-versed in goalkeeping. Consequently, young goalies must often coach themselves. To analyze your own performance, you need to know the mechanics of your position. Here are some pointers:

1. The two considerations of angle play are remaining equidistant to the imaginary lines drawn from the ball to both posts while being as far off your line as possible without making yourself vulnerable to being chipped. The visual clue allowing you to extend your range is a ball that's rolling your way—because it's extremely difficult for a shooter to dip a ball that's rolling toward the goal. Conversely, a ball rolling diagonally or toward the shooter is a warning to stand within the range at which you can safely cover your crossbar.

2. Be a "big man on campus." Playing angles aggressively makes an attacker more likely to pass than to shoot. And if that player does shoot, he is more likely to be off-target.

3. When a shot is forthcoming, hop forward into your stance, with your weight on the balls of your feet and your knees bent so that your body is prepared to spring in any direction. Your eyes are riveted on the ball. If you're close to the shooter, your center of gravity and hands should be lower.

4. Your hands should always lead your body to the ball.

5. Whenever possible, dive forward to meet the ball. When diving to your right, take a power step with your right foot that is to your right *and* forward. Milutin Soskic—the U.S. National Team's goalkeeper coach and himself a former international keeper—tells me that failing to do this is one of the most common shortcomings he sees among young goalies.

6. Make sure that your hands work together to form the W. As you catch a ball in midair, it should be rotated toward the field of play. Thus, when diving to your right, the ball moves in a counterclockwise direction (clockwise for a dive to your left). The near-sided hand moves from behind the ball to being more toward its top. Your hands are at approximately 10 o'clock and 2 o'clock as the ball meets the ground before your body to help lessen the impact of your dive.

Fig. 8.2. Great technique from Brazil's Taffarel: His hands form the W, his body is behind the ball, his far-side knee drives across his body to increase his diving range, and his eyes are riveted on the ball.

7. Whenever possible, position your body to provide a back-up surface in case your hands should fail. If it's feasible, taking the ball against your chest is preferable.

8. On low shots struck at you, cradle the ball into your chest. Get your upper body over the ball as you dive forward to meet it and watch the ball into your hands (pulling your head up as the ball arrives might cause you to fumble it).

9. Ground balls shot to either side entail getting your near-sided hand low early and letting that hand lead your body into the dive. Use your far-sided hand to come over the top to help trap the ball against the turf.

10. Ground balls hit firmly a few feet to either side require you to collapse to the ground. If the ball is to your right, your right foot kicks out to your left. Your hands should reach the ground first as your body falls downward.

11. When boxing a ball at the near post, use two hands to punch it back in the general direction it came from. For any ball on which you must retreat, your near-sided hand comes around the back and underside of the ball to propel it in the same direction in which it was

© Jon Van Woerden

Fig. 8.3. Low shots aren't the only ones that you can grasp against your chest. Notice how Jorge Campos cradles the ball while flying through the air.

headed. Regardless of your aiming point, the order of your priorities is always to hit the ball high, wide, and far.

12. One always-difficult play is when you must dive into feet to block a shot that's launched before you can get to the ball. Time your move to hit the ground as the ball is struck. You must be close enough to the shooter that she has no time to react. The imaginary line drawn from the ball to the goal's center is bisected by your chest, with your hands toward the near-post side. Use your far-sided arm to come

across your face for protection. Get both hands as close to the ball as possible as it leaves the shooter's foot.

13. Advance forward in a one-on-one (breakaway) situation only *between* the attacker's touches. Don't be caught in stride as the attacker is contacting the ball or she will exploit your inability to change direction at that instant. Your visual clue is to look for a long stray touch that allows you to race forward to win the ball. If the attacker keeps the ball under close control, proceed with caution. Keep your knees bent and your hands close to the ground with your palms facing the ball.

Should an attacker try to dribble you, it's preferable to force her toward the near post, which is guarded by your hands. All you need to do is get a touch to redirect the ball out of the attacker's path or to force her to dribble so far wide of you at speed that maintaining control is virtually impossible. By forcing the attacker wide, you can get help from the goal line or from a defender who races back to cover behind you.

Most attackers prefer to go around the side guarded by your hands, as the risk of being kicked isn't appealing. By slightly angling your approach to show a bit more of the near post, you can further entice them to go in that direction.

14. Crosses should be collected at the highest possible point. Bring your knee up both for protection and to increase the force with which you leap. For balls being played in from wide positions, your body should be open to the field, and you should be as far back in the goal as possible without exposing the near post (since it's always easier for you to take two steps forward than to take one step backward).

Know the referee. In Britain, a robust challenge on the keeper is considered part of the game, whereas goalies in Italy receive a great deal of protection. These differences affect your decision about whether to try to catch a cross or box it away. Kasey Keller of Millwall learned this lesson. Millwall was eliminated from a Cup competition after losing a 1-0 heartbreaker on a late goal in which Kasey felt that he had been fouled by a hard-charging forward who initiated the contact that caused Keller to drop the ball.

Kasey now knows that, when in doubt, opt for safety first. But he also knows that, in most places, a foul would have been called and the opposing forward might have found his name in the referee's book.

15. There was a time when awarding a penalty kick was considered an almost automatic goal. Today's keepers force the shooter to

strike a near-perfect shot in order to score. Goalies today take advantage of their athleticism, technique, and, equally important, the tendency of many referees to allow them to move early during a penalty kick.

There are two schools of thought when dealing with penalties. One theory is that you should read the shooter's hips and/or foot position for clues and then react to the shot. The other theory is to guess where the ball will be aimed and to move accordingly. I feel that a penalty kick tie-breaker presents a different set of circumstances than the awarding of a penalty kick during a match. One or two of five tie-breaker participants will likely produce a subpar kick. But during a game the opponents will select their most efficient penalty taker. The odds are that the ball will be struck firmly and well-placed. In this situation your best chance at making a save is to guess correctly and move early.

Not everyone would agree with me. Brad Friedel, at six feet, four inches, and with long arms and an explosive dive, is able to get his fingertips on balls that most keepers couldn't hope to reach. Brad's preference, then, is to wait to dive until the last possible split-second to try to uncover any clues that he gets from reading the shooter. Because of his extraordinary attributes, Brad can use a strategy that won't work for many goalies. It's up to you to get to know your own strengths and weaknesses before devising an approach that best suits you.

As you may know, regular penalty takers tend to be confident and quite clever. They often try to disguise their intentions. A tie-breaker involves several shooters, many of whom are not accustomed to being in that situation. They are more likely to miss the target, underhit the ball, or place it too close to the keeper. If you can prevent even one attempt from entering your net, that could be enough to win. In that situation, you may decide that trying to react to the shot is your best option.

When it comes to defending tie-breakers, it helps to know your opponent's history. Argentina has a good record in tie-breakers but Mexico has had an awful run of luck. We were well aware of that when we beat them via the tie-breaker in the quarterfinal round of the 1995 Copa America. Brad made two great reaction saves and all four of our shooters scored.

As one of the penalty takers, I must admit that Jorge Campos's lack of size gave me extra confidence that if I hit the ball well there would be no way he could get to it. I'm not so sure I would have felt as comfortable had I been staring at Argentina's Sergio Goycochea, who was only beaten a combined five times in successive tie-breakers that lifted his country past Yugoslavia and Italy in the 1990 World Cup. Sergio made some amazing saves on seemingly well-taken shots. The combination of his reputation and stature also induced some opponents into substandard efforts.

As a keeper during a penalty kick or a tie-breaker, your aura is key. Do whatever you can prior to the kick to make yourself appear larger than you are. Wave your arms. Hop up and down. Stand upright. Make that attacker think that anything less than a perfect shot won't suffice. Putting that element of doubt in his mind could be enough to make him feel that he must strike the ball with full force and aim just inches inside of a post.

Even with better goalkeeping, the number one cause of missed penalty kicks owes to the shooter changing his or her mind at the last instant. Knowing this, I try not to pay any attention to what the keeper is doing. I know he's trying to make me change my mind by giving the appearance that he's going to dive in one specific direction (many goalies "throw" an arm outward as a distraction just before the ball is struck). But ignoring the keeper's actions comes under the easier-said-than-done category. As a goalie, you should do what you can (within the bounds of good sportsmanship) to throw off the shooter.

Regardless of whether you guess or react, the technical aspect is the same. Your first step is with the leg on the side to which you will dive. When diving to your right, your right foot steps forward and slightly sideways with your toes pointed at two o'clock. You explode off that foot into a dive that is slightly forward.

16. Be aggressive. You want to avoid miscalculations, but it's far better to make two aggressive mistakes such as coming for balls just out of your range than to make one passive error such as refusing to deal with a cross that's well within reach. Think of things from the attacker's perspective. Finishing is difficult enough without having some keeper charging like an angry rhinoceros in your direction. That opponent is far less likely to be composed when put under pressure.

Of course this isn't to suggest that you should come for every ball. Let your defenders deal with balls out of your reach. But, when in doubt, it's far better to make an aggressive decision. Always remember that the objective of playing isn't to avoid making a mistake. The idea is to do something positive. Negative thoughts almost always lead to negative results. Positive and assertive play is far more likely to lead to positive results.

17. When receiving any ball from one side of the field, look immediately to the opposite side to ascertain your best distribution option.

As a goalkeeper, it's better to make two aggressive mistakes than one passive mistake.

18. Reserve drop-kicks for when you're facing a strong wind or when you need to get a ball quickly and relatively accurately to a teammate who is out of range of a throw. For a drop-kick, drop the ball in front of you and slightly to the side. Strike it as close to the ground as possible. Lock your ankle so that your toes remain pointed downward long after booting the ball. For obvious reasons, do not try a drop-kick on a muddy or frozen pitch.

19. Your drop of the ball is an important but often overlooked factor in your being able to consistently punt for distance and accuracy. Your release should be with the hand that's on the same side as your kicking foot. Drop the ball gently (don't throw it forward or to the side). Lock your ankle with your toes pointed downward. Explode through the ball and land on your kicking foot.

20. Always remember that you're no better than your defense in front of you. It's your job to keep them organized and confident. Pay attention to what is happening off the ball. Quite often, danger lurks on the weakside. The proper positioning of your defenders is key.

When the ball is wide to your right, the left fullback should be deeper (closer to the goal line) than the opponents' right wing. That fullback is pinched well into a central position to be able to provide cover for a teammate who may be beaten while also being able to cover that wing should a cross be put in. As the ball is worked back across the middle, that defender must close down the space to the player he is assigned to mark.

In figure 8.4, the attacking left midfielder has the ball 40 yards from the goal. From that distance you can come just beyond the 6-yard box to cut out any long balls over the top of your defense while still being close enough to your line to get any chipped shot. Your weakside defender, X_5, is pinched toward the middle and is both in the path to your goal of the attacking right wing and able to provide cover if needed should X_3 be beaten by the opposing striker. The sweeper, X_4, is able to provide cover behind both X_2 and X_3. If the ball is played across the midfield, X_2 will drop while X_5 moves closer to the right wing.

There is no such thing as a strictly man-to-man or zone defense. Zonal systems always incorporate some form of marking and man-to-man systems require those in covering positions to employ zonal principles to help out and cover for their teammates when necessary.

Flat back fours call for that weakside defender to be on the same plane as his or her mates. If that's your system, remember that the defender must still pinch in toward the ball. The gaps between defenders must be sufficiently small to prevent penetration. Your objective is to make sure that all the attacking team's passes/moves go in front of and around your defense and never through them.

In coachspeak, the changing roles of players as the ball is passed calls for "first attackers" (who are marked by "first defenders"), "second attackers" (guarded by "second defenders"), and "third attackers"

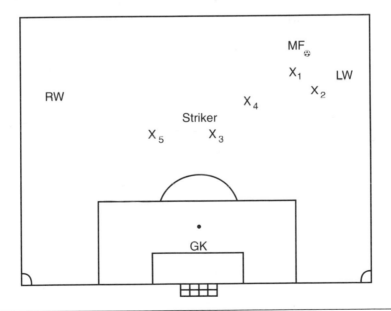

Fig. 8.4. Organizing the defense ranks high on the list of important goalkeeper chores. Here the opposing midfielder has the ball 40 years from the goal. The defenders are properly positioned to provide cover for teammates who may be beaten.

(with third defenders assigned to them while also being ready to cover for a second defender).

The first attacker is the player with the ball. Second attackers are those in immediate support positions; there should be a player to either side and at least another in front of the first attacker. The second attackers move toward the ball to provide immediate support. Third attackers are charged with creating space for their mates to spread the field. They can also make dangerous penetrating runs to get on the end of a long cross-field pass.

Your first defender's job is to close the first attacker. By getting within tackling distance, the first defender hopes to force that foe to look down at the ball and thus lose vision. Another objective is to jockey that attacker either toward another defender (to win the ball back) or at least in the direction presenting the least danger.

Second defenders must mark their respective opponents. The gaps between them should always be smaller than those between the first and second attackers. Third defenders provide what coaches refer to as "balance."

When the ball is played upfield your defenders push up in the direction of the ball. This isn't to be confused with an offside trap. But, in both cases, it's essential that there be immediate pressure on the ball lest a withdrawn attacker dash though a gap to latch onto a through ball.

You need to know the basic principles of defending if you are to perform your role as a coach on the field. The quality (or lack thereof) of instructions you provide is as important a duty as making saves. As the only player on your team who can see the entire field and all the other 21 players, your leadership is vital.

GOALKEEPER'S PRACTICE SESSION

A typical warm-up includes stretching and then some "soft hands" work. The keepers in figure 8.5 are balancing their bodies with two feet and one arm. They toss the ball back and forth using one hand, with palm down and fingers up. The stance can be on one's heels/palm or in a push-up-like position. Either way, the catching hand must give as the ball arrives so that it can be held.

Next, sit on your butt with your feet together and directly in front of you. Your partner serves grounders from a few yards away, kicking shots to either side. Try to be technically correct as you simultaneously bring both hands to the ball. Don't lazily make a one-handed

a

b

© Steve Slade

Fig. 8.5. From either of these positions, the "soft hands" drill helps to improve your hand-eye coordination and your ability to hold onto the ball.

catch just because the shots are so slow that you can get away with it. Remember—practice only improves your skills if you practice doing things the right way.

Ease into your diving by having your partner serve balls either out of his or her hands or via a punt from approximately five yards away. Start on your knees, move to a crouch, and work your way up to the real thing.

Afterward, lie on the ground with the server standing above you. As you perform a sit-up, the server drops a ball to either side of your ankles. Make the save and return the ball quickly. The next ball is then served above your head. Catch it and lie down before repeating the action.

A similar exercise starts with your lying on your side. Using one ball, the server tosses it so that you must thrust upward with your waist to make the catch. Your hands go to the ball (they aren't permitted to push your body off the ground). You'll find this exercise improves your conditioning as well as your technique.

A somewhat more vigorous exercise is illustrated in Figure 8.6, below. Here, you must make a diving save over a kneeling partner.

Fig. 8.6. In this exercise, the server (foreground) aims an underhand toss high and wide of the kneeling obstacle person. As you make the two-handed save, land on the side of your body with the ball impacting the ground first. Make sure to work on diving to both your left and your right while maintaining proper technique throughout.

Begin the exercise standing on one side of your partner, who is on all fours. After the server has tossed the ball to the opposite side of your partner, you attempt to catch it cleanly in midair using both hands simultaneously as you dive over your partner. Keep your body square to the ball throughout the dive. As always, your hands should move to the ball first, with your body immediately following. Try to rotate the ball slightly after catching it so that your hands are at the 10 o'clock and 2 o'clock positions as the ball impacts the grounds just before you land. Then cradle the ball into your chest. This exercise is normally done in sets of 10 serves.

Now that you're warmed up, here are some more two-ball drills to try:

• The server stands at the 18-yard line and tosses the first ball underhand. You race out to catch it before it hits the ground. Return it to the server, who then chips a shot over your head. You retreat at speed and either catch the ball (if possible) or turn your body so that the hand closer to the server comes around and under the ball to tip it over the crossbar.

• Try the same thing except that the first ball is tapped on the ground. You must fly off your line to dive on the ball. Once again, the second serve is lofted.

• Try the same sort of drills only with the server wide of the six-yard box. The first ball is short and the second one is chipped.

• A passive attacker dribbles the ball into the box. You come off your line to win the ball. You then leap to your feet to face a shot from a server who is positioned behind and slightly to the side of the player who was just dispossessed.

• One server is on the penalty spot and a second server is behind the goal. The former takes a shot that can be saved. As you recover, turn to catch a ball that the server from behind the goal tosses just over the crossbar. As always, you should catch the ball at the highest possible point.

At St. Pauli, we did this exercise with the server positioned behind the goal. The keeper sits on the ground and must get to his feet quickly to catch the ball as it is over (or just beyond) the crossbar. The ball is returned and the action repeats.

• Two servers, with a few balls apiece, stand at the top of the penalty box and opposite a goalpost. They alternate taking shots. You must make a save, recover to your feet, and scramble to find the best angle for the subsequent shot.

© Dan Herbst

Fig. 8.7. U.S. National Team Goalkeeper Coach Milutin Soskic puts Brad Friedel through the paces on the day before a match at Washington's RFK Stadium. In this exercise, Brad lies on his left side. "Scholey" flips the ball so that Brad just lifts himself up without pushing off the ground with his hands before making the save.

Obviously, the three keepers take turns serving. When you're in serving, remember that these exercises are done for the benefit of the keeper. Don't attempt to score only to sail balls high, wide, and far. Instead, hit your shots to force the goalie to make a full-stretch diving save. And don't shoot before the keeper is ready. The more purposeful work that everyone gets, the better you'll all become.

• Servers are positioned just inside of the right and left touchlines about 20 to 30 yards from the goal line. Each has several balls. The first server pushes a ball forward, prepares it toward the goal, looks up, and strikes a cross. If it's within your range, attempt to catch it at its highest point. If you can take it cleanly, turn and throw it to the opposite server. If you box it away, the second server uses one of the spare balls. Either way, run back to your starting point before the second server crosses the ball.

Your progression is to add an attacker (or two) in the box to challenge for balls. Don't get in bad habits by chasing crosses outside your range. And add a rule that the central attackers receiving such a ball must shoot on the first touch. On every cross yell either "keeper" or "away!" An alternative to facing crosses is to work with a server and a passive opponent (as shown in figure 8.8).

As Bernie Watt has noted, not many young keepers are sufficiently schooled to cope with crosses. In the pros a goalie will usually face far more crosses than shots. Thus, deficiencies in this area will severely limit how far you'll go as a keeper.

- Here are a couple of somersault drills:

  1. Stand a few yards in front of one post, facing the opposite post. The server is on the penalty spot with several balls. You initiate the action by completing a forward roll. Hop to your feet and assume your stance. The ball is then shot along the ground toward the far post. Make the save, discard the ball, and move to a few yards in front of that post while facing the opposite way. Do this exercise in sets of eight to ten saves.

Fig. 8.8. In this drill the server tosses the ball over the head of a passive attacker. Time your leap to catch the ball at its highest point. Take care to keep the ball from hitting the opponent's head, lest you drop it (if you sense that danger exists, it may be best to box the ball to safety).

2. To hone your reactions, start on your line in the middle of the goal. The server again has several balls. This time he is positioned between the penalty spot and the center of the six-yard line. Do a front roll, which should bring you to within five yards of the server. Just as you come to your feet, the server powerfully punts a ball either at you or a yard (at most) to either side. In this case, feel free to parry the ball although, as always, catch anything that you can. Do this drill in sets of eight to ten saves.

Given the pace of the shots and the proximity of the players, use your common sense when serving. Take care not to strike shots at delicate body parts and use only hand-stitched balls that aren't overinflated.

• Another reaction situation has a server standing on the goal line a few feet wide of the post. A shooter is on the six-yard line about even with the near post. You, the keeper, begin on the line in the position you'd assume if that server was a live player in a game situation. The server passes on the ground to the shooter, who must strike the ball on the first touch. It's your job to make yourself as "big" as possible by quickly narrowing the angle. Keep a low enough stance to deal with the subsequent shot.

A variation of this drill is to toss the serve underhand and for the shooter to hit a side- or full-volley. This makes it even more imperative that you move aggressively off your line. However, this time keep your stance and hands higher than when dealing with a shot struck from the turf (see figure 8.9).

GO TO WAR!

The highlight of almost any goalkeeper camp is competing at Goalie Wars. This game is played several ways, the most common being to have two full-sized goals about 18 to 20 yards apart with a healthy supply of spare balls inside each.

One keeper begins play with a shot. The other goalie tries to make the save. If it's caught cleanly, that ball can then be immediately thrown, punted, or drop-kicked. If the ball was parried, the keeper making the save grabs another ball out of his net and takes a shot. To emphasize clean handling, you may decide to stipulate that the original shooter gets to shoot again when the opposing keeper only parries the ball. This will force you to attempt to catch the difficult shot.

Fig. 8.9. Assume an angle to defend against a shot from the server (right). As soon as the ball is kicked or tossed to the player who is volleying the ball, move across the goal before attempting to make the save.

Goalie Wars can also be played using a couple of milk crates with a stick across the top of them. The two goals should be no more than 12 yards apart and about half to two-thirds the size of a regulation goal (use cones, shirts, or corner flags to serve as your goalposts). All shots are thrown, with you having to skip the ball under the stick and between the crates. Play to 11 or 15 goals; the winner must win by at least 2.

Goalie War tournaments are a blast. More important, the amount of action really improves your fitness while constantly challenging your techniques.

GAME-RELATED PRACTICE EXERCISES

By the nature of the job, goalkeepers are accustomed to practicing on their own or with one or two compatriots. You have probably found or created several drills that have become your favorites. I have offered suggestions for you to consider, but I do think the best training for goalkeepers is to play in small-sided games in appropriately sized spaces with regulation goals. Many of the games described in the previous two chapters can do more for you than any five drills.

I do not mean to denigrate the value of working on your own or with a friend or two. Repetitive practice on the many types of saves you must make is necessary to acquire and retain proper technique. But it's not always the keeper with the best form or who best looks the part who turns out being the best goalie. For example, many people would dismiss Campos as being too short to play at a high level. But his positional sense, field player skills, leaping ability, and intangibles (confidence, intelligence, and determination) have made him a bona fide star. I know of others whose techniques are far from perfect but whose personalities are top-notch. Assuming you have a degree of skill, it's the possession of outstanding psychological parameters that's most important for your development.

That's why maintaining a proper perspective is an absolute must. So is gaining experience in match-realistic situations. The small-sided game forces you to make decisions. Here are some you might try:

• I'm partial to 4-v-4 up to 7-v-7. Fewer than four field players per side allows for too much time and space, which makes finishing situations false. Too many players either makes the field too crowded to be realistic or requires such a large surface that scoring chances are few and far between.

• Whenever the game is 5-v-5 or bigger, try adding a neutral player or two. This encourages quick ball movement for the attackers and gives them more and a greater variety of situations to try to finish. It also forces defenders to compact and make good, quick decisions.

• A great game to play is 6-v-4 on a 40- to 50-yard long field. The team of six attacks a full-sized goal with a keeper. The numbers-down side tries to score on two smaller goals (without a keeper) placed a few yards inside of each touchline. The positioning of those goals reminds defenders to play the ball wide whenever possible as they try to get out of their own third.

• Indoor soccer is great for honing your reactions, but it's also somewhat false—especially if you play on a hockey-style rink with goals built into the endboards. You'll certainly improve your ability to dive into feet and to block point-blank blasts, but you're quite likely to get in the bad habit of parrying shots. You'll find that you need to adjust when you go back outdoors and have to deal with crosses and an eight-foot high crossbar again.

Still, indoor soccer is far better than no soccer. It's certainly a good way to remain active in the game for those of you who live in areas where the climate isn't conducive to year-round outdoor play.

FINAL THOUGHTS

From Goalie Wars to two-ball drills, there are more useful keeper-related activities now than ever before. The advent of specialization coaches and camps gives keepers access to quality instruction that's far superior to what we had a generation ago. As helpful as they all are, your best route is to play as often as possible in small-sided games.

Watch as many high-level games live as you can. To get a better understanding of defensive principles, study what occurs off the ball. Make notes of how keepers organize their defenses and their positioning in various situations. These are vital aspects of the game that aren't seen within the range of the TV camera.

Seek out the advice of your heroes. When Tony Meola was growing up in New Jersey, he was taken under the wing of then New York Cosmos star Hubert Birkenmeier. Hubert became something of a personal instructor/coach to Tony and was instrumental in Tony's rise to becoming one of the finest keepers in U.S. soccer history. One of Tony's finest assets is his resiliency, a crucial trait for a goalkeeper.

Every player makes mistakes. You will, too. Unfortunately, as the goalie, you are the only athlete on the field whose errors are immediately posted on the scoreboard. It's how you respond to that which will determine if you have what it takes to be a great keeper.

CHAPTER

9

Developing the Attitude of a Winner

"Soccer is about we, not me."

While improving your skills is vital, it's even more important to have the right priorities. All of us have individual goals, and this is fine as long as all conflicts between your personal ambitions and those of the team are resolved in favor of the latter. From reading newspapers and magazines, you may have a distorted view regarding the attitude that characterizes the vast majority of top-class athletes. For every misfit out there, there are scores who abide by the rules and conduct themselves as ambassadors for their sport. Your attitude and how you deal with setbacks will determine how far you'll get in your sport. Several talented players have had their careers short-circuited by their inability to control their egos and emotions.

There is a certain mentality in soccer that I find admirable. Even with the fiercely competitive nature of the game, there remains a high degree of sportsmanship. Soccer players routinely boot balls into touch so that an injured opponent may receive treatment. We still return the ball on the subsequent restart to the team that intentionally halted play. There's a genuine respect that rivals have for each other. You'll have to watch a lot of games to catch soccer players engaging in trash talk.

Take time to consider the examples cited in this chapter of how you ought to behave on and off the soccer field. Honestly evaluate how you relate to teammates, coaches, opponents, referees, and the game itself. If you don't give yourself high marks, know that it's not too late to improve your attitude. And realize that your attitude is every bit as key to your success as your speed, skill, tactical awareness, and enjoyment of the sport.

RESPECTING YOUR OPPONENTS

After competing with every ounce of nationalistic pride that one can muster for 90 minutes, international games conclude with athletes embracing as they exchange their jerseys in a ritual that illustrates the level of respect these players harbor for their worthy opponents. They are an adversary who you try your best to defeat, but at no time are they viewed as an enemy.

An opponent is not an enemy.

Carry yourself with class in victory and dignity in defeat. Don't brag when you win or offer excuses when you lose. Regardless of the outcome, show respect for those you competed against. There's no place in sports for running up scores, belittling others, being obnoxiously arrogant, or mouthing off.

Every minute you're on that field you should play with full commitment. Always compete with yourself to become the best player that your natural talents will allow. If you slack off because your team has a big lead or falls hopelessly behind, that's when you stop improving.

DEALING WITH REFEREES

I'm quite proud to be held in generally high regard by referees (I think!). I was well into my second decade of professional soccer before I was sent off for the first time. Before being critical of a referee, consider that it would be impossible for us to enjoy playing this great game if it weren't for a group of people who so love the sport that they're willing to perform a thankless task for very little (if any) compensation. The ref is the only person on the field who is expected to be perfect when the match begins (and to improve as the game progresses!). Try to imagine that you scored five goals in a game and not a single person stopped to praise you. That's how a referee feels after doing a great job. But let that same individual make a mistake— or even display the courage to make a tough call in a key situation— and players and fans are sure to howl in protest.

I enter every game knowing that I will do my best to avoid mistakes, but that some will inevitably occur. Why, then, should I expect the referee to be flawless? As long as that official is working hard to keep up with the play and is doing his or her best, that's all that any of us can reasonably expect. Yes, there will be times when a dodgy awarding of a penalty seemingly decides a match. This happened to our National Team in Sweden in a 1995 friendly. In the 86th minute Martin Dahlin performed a dive worthy of Greg Louganis. Tomas Brolin calmly strolled to the spot and spoiled a fantastic nine-save performance by Brad Friedel by scoring the evening's only goal. In such a situation it's very easy to point fingers at the referee. But doing so, in my opinion, is both faulty match analysis and a copout. Nobody would have remembered that call had we scored twice in that game. As athletes, it's our job to figure out what we must do better next time to win. And then we must work on those aspects to improve, both individually and collectively.

Players who lose their composure over a controversial call are often a detriment to their team. Losing your cool is usually silly and almost always counterproductive. As a defender, I know which forwards easily become distracted. I gain a great edge the moment that their concentration wavers. A player's displayed anger can alienate the referee. That person with the whistle is every bit as human as are you. As much as an official tries not to be swayed by the personalities of the participants, only the most extraordinary referee is able to fully block out such considerations. If you constantly whine or dive at every minor contact, don't expect many 50-50 calls to go your way.

As a player, you don't have the time to be worrying about calls made by the referee. Playing at a high level demands constant focus and concentration. There are only three things that a person can do on a soccer field: play, coach, or referee—and if you try to do more than one of these at a time you'll almost certainly play poorly.

© Jon Van Woerden

Fig. 9.1. Chances are, this man loves the game as much as you or I do. At the very least, his dedication and position should be enough to earn your respect.

What should you do when the opponents score a goal on a play in which everyone but the referee and referee's assistant (linesperson) saw that they were obviously offside? Step one: Calm down any of your teammates so that nobody makes a bad situation worse by alienating the ref or getting cautioned or sent off. Step two: rally your team together by telling them, "What's done is done. Let's forget about it and find a way to get that goal back." Players and teams that don't whine and curse when a call goes against them will gain the respect of opponents, the media, and, yes, the referees.

There have been times when I have quietly approached a referee with a concern regarding an opponent's actions. I've found that most officials will hear me out and are receptive to my concerns as long as I present them respectfully. Here are the ground rules I've established regarding communication with refs:

1. I always ask the ref's permission before calling anything to his or her attention. If permission is denied, I drop the issue and concentrate on playing the game.

2. I never make an obvious approach that alerts the fans that I have a beef. Arguing visibly with a ref is certain to get the fans booing, which is hardly a way to ingratiate yourself to an official.

3. I try not to speak while I'm still angry. It's far better to wait until I know that I can communicate in a polite and respectful manner.

4. I don't question a decision that's already been made. If I must second-guess, I usually say something like, "Could you please try to make sure that all future challenges by their number seven are made with his studs down."

5. I find that humor helps, as long as it isn't sarcastic. For example, you might say, "Please be sure to call their offsides because I'm too slow to catch those guys from behind!"

6. I also find that empathy usually helps. "I know it's impossible for one person to see everything, but I'd appreciate it if you could alert your linesmen to keep an eye out for their number nine doing some pushing off the ball. Thank you."

7. Now and then I find myself engaged in damage control—especially after a teammate has made some ill-advised comments. More than once I've pulled a teammate away from a

heated situation to prevent his being sent off. That accomplished, I might tell the ref that he or she had made a good call and not to worry about it. Believe me, soccer is difficult enough without antagonizing the individual in charge of calling the match.

8. After I have expressed a concern, I always thank the ref for listening. That isn't a line of bull. I appreciate it when an official is open-minded enough to consider my viewpoint.

9. I never make refs feel that they've lost control of a match. Showing confidence in their ability allows them to do a better job. They experience the same emotions that players do, which means they also need to hear an occasional compliment.

Fig. 9.2. Germany's Rudi Voller (left) hasn't been behaving himself. Note the respectful and nonthreatening body language of Captain Lothar Matthaus as he waits for the right moment to say something on his teammate's behalf.

10. I try to read the situation. There are some times when the best words are no words.

Contrary to popular misconceptions, referees are *not* responsible for the game's outcome. Matches are won and lost by players, not by refs and linespeople. When a decision occurs, honestly evaluate what you and your teammates could (and should) have done better. Whenever you blame the referee you're being a poor sport and, perhaps more important, you're missing the opportunity to learn from mistakes you and your team made in the match. I've never heard a member of a winning team credit a ref for their victory. Until that occurs, it's unfair to blame them for a defeat.

DEALING WITH THOSE IN THE SAME-COLORED SHIRT AS YOU

Never forget that soccer is a team game. No player wins a match on his or her own, and no one player can ever be responsible for a defeat. Take, for example, a 30-yard shot that sails harmlessly through the air only to slip through your keeper's hands. Is your goalie culpable? Absolutely. But let's not forget that someone on your team had to lose possession of the ball in the first place (which could have also been the fault of players nearby not moving into intelligent supporting positions). After the ball was lost, someone was responsible for allowing the opponents to penetrate. And who left the shooter so wide open for that shot?

Team responsibility was a constant theme of Bora Milutinovic. After games leading up to the 1994 World Cup, he'd quiz us on why each goal had been conceded. We would then study tapes. He'd rewind the tape back to when we first lost possession. Almost without exception, those goals resulted from a succession of errors.

Bora's assistant coach, Timo Liekoski, often reminded us that soccer is a turnover sport in which reacting quickly in transition is important. He stressed that following a turnover we should make every effort not to allow the other team to make an immediate penetrating pass. But that's exactly what happened on a considerable percentage of goals that we analyzed.

Always look in the mirror after a loss and ask yourself, "What could I have done better to help the team?" Think "me" after a loss and "we" after a win. If you score the winning goal, make a point to credit others for the role they played to provide you with that opportunity. You'll find that the more credit you deflect, the more will come back to you. Conversely, the more blame you dish out, the less respect you'll get (and deserve) from teammates and coaches.

Soccer is a game of mistakes, and I've certainly made my share. One of my first and worst errors occurred in the annual Milk Cup match that pitted the Under-19 State teams of Northern and Southern California. Our team led 2-1 late in the match when yours truly tied the contest with an own goal. One of my teammates was beaten on the dribble in the box. I jumped up to block the shot, only to have the ball hit the side of my head and deflect into the net. I suppose I could have pointed the finger at the teammate who had been beaten, but I knew that if I hadn't turned my body, the ball would have hit me squarely.

Yes, I was unlucky. But I flinched, and my doing so cost us the game. Afterward, I apologized to my teammates for turning my back on the ball. To a man, they were very supportive. Most of them said, "Don't worry about it Paul—we all lost this game together."

I received a lot of credit for the goal against Trinidad. But it's a mistake when anyone says or writes that it was my play that got us into the 1990 World Cup. We wouldn't have gotten to Italy if our defense hadn't produced four consecutive shutouts in qualifying. Nor would we have made it if not for the goals scored by other Americans in the previous games. We qualified as a team, together. Never forget that TEAM stands for "Together Everyone Achieves More."

At my level, it's very easy for outside forces to harm team unity. For example, players who score goals or have marketable personalities tend to get more publicity than others who may actually contribute more to their club's success. This can be a problem for players who covet glory. My perspective is that I'm extremely fortunate to be able to play pro soccer. Moreover, I'd far rather be a role player on a winning team than the so-called star on a losing team. If you crave individual honors, you should be playing an individual sport like golf, tennis, or bowling.

There's no more emotional moment in sports than every four years when the winning team lifts the World Cup. Even through the TV you can feel the unbridled passion those athletes are experiencing while members of the losing team sink to their knees in despair when the final whistle blows. To see grown-ups reduced to tears of

© Jon Van Woerden

Fig. 9.3. You want to know how intense soccer is at the top level? Check out the faces of your National Team members while we defend a free kick during Italia '90. From left: Tab Ramos, Marcelo Balboa, myself, Bruce Murray, John Harkes, and Peter Vermes.

ecstasy or agony says volumes about what really matters in a team sport.

Even if you or I never experience that, I can guarantee you that decades from now we'll still feel a special sense of pride and accomplishment from having been a part of a successful team. The matter of which player is named all-league or all-section should be irrelevant. More times than I can count, I've heard an athlete named his or her sport's MVP declare the desire to share that honor with his or her teammates. Such statements may sound trite, but they are almost always sincere.

As far as I'm concerned, there's no problem if Alexi Lalas or Cobi Jones gets more publicity than do I. Their appearances on *The Tonight Show* and MTV only help to increase soccer awareness in the U.S. That's good for the game and for all of us who play the sport. Accept that certain players will get a disproportionate amount of attention from outsiders. Don't ever doubt that your contributions are not fully valued by the only people who truly matter—your coaches, your teammates, and yourself.

© Jon Van Woerden

Fig. 9.4. Playing all-out while maintaining your composure isn't easy. During his great career in the USA and Europe, John Harkes has proven that you can battle for every ball without losing your cool.

Like referees, teammates will make mistakes. Don't ever let a mistake cause an argument as play is continuing. Sort it out afterward in the locker room in a positive way. Or, after a play has ended and before the action has restarted, briefly discuss with the teammate what both of you will do in a similar situation in the future. Always be positive. Don't assign blame. What's done is done. The most important play in soccer is the next play, as it's the only play that you can affect.

There are times when you must be a leader. If you see two of your teammates engaged in a heated disagreement, you should tell them to get on with the job. Later on, try to help them resolve their dispute. If you're unsuccessful, enlist the help of your captain or, if

The most important play is the next play.
—Bora Milutinovic

necessary, your coach. If a resentment between teammates is allowed to fester it can become a cancer that will significantly harm your team.

I think it's fair to claim with pride that our 1994 World Cup Team overachieved. We shocked the mighty Colombians (who Pele had predicted would lift the trophy) because we alone believed that we could beat them. We tied the Swiss by coming together against a European opponent that, man-for-man, had superior talent and experience to our own.

That same winning attitude we had on the National Team I had encountered years before at UCLA. No Bruin cared about who got the credit. Guys who had been stars for their club and school teams were willing to be role players. Everyone was given a specific function by coach Sigi Schmid. We all knew and understood our own roles and those of our teammates. We warmed up together. We cooled down together. Heck, we even studied for exams together. And we worked hard.

One example of our winning attitude came from a preseason training session, where our endurance was pushed to the limit. We were divided into two groups and were in the ninth of ten shuttle runs, each of which had to be finished in 30 seconds or less. If not, our entire group would have to run some more. In one of the groups were two players who couldn't get over the finish line in time. As they staggered down the backstretch, each was helped by a faster teammate who literally half-pushed, half-carried them over the line. The guys doing the assisting were future USA National Team members Dale Ervine and Paul Krumpe. The slower members just couldn't make the final shuttle, so their group had to run again. The group that wasn't required to run decided to join them to show support for their teammates. That is how our 1985 season began, and that's how it ended—with unity.

Three months later, we faced American University in the Seattle Kingdome in the NCAA Division I Final. It was our first game in three years on artificial turf. Both sides were technical teams that liked to work the ball up the field with short passes. The surface didn't do either team's attacking players any favors. Our edge was that we found solutions to every challenge. In the semifinal we had worn gloves in the freezing cold at Evansville while their players, acclimated to the conditions, played in shorts.

In the Final, neither side had many offensive opportunities in regulation time. The game remained scoreless. We played an overtime period. Still no goals. Two overtimes. And then three, four, five, six, and seven. Midnight came and went. Players on both squads were fully exhausted. Not until the eighth extra period did the most unlikely of heroes emerge.

Andy Burke hadn't scored in his college career. He was well-liked and respected for how he continued to work hard in practice and for being a positive influence on the team despite receiving limited playing time. It would have been easy for Andy to grouch about not being used more by Sigi. We all know of players in that situation who blame politics for their fate. Instead, Andy worked very hard to improve his weaknesses. Of those, a less-than-sensational left foot had been his most glaring shortcoming.

In that eighth overtime of the final game, Paul Krumpe had the ball near where the midfield line and the right touchline intersect. Our attacking midfielder, Dale Ervine, made a penetrating run. Paul's long pass was flicked ever-so-slightly by Dale. Andy controlled the ball with his first touch before volleying it just inside the far post. And—you guessed it—not only did Andy score the only goal of the championship game, he did it with his left foot!

Given the nature of that team, for which a different hero stepped up every game, maybe that was the most likely of conclusions. I know this for sure: I wouldn't own an NCAA championship ring if Andy Burke wasn't such a great person who put his team's needs ahead of his own.

HANDLING DISAPPOINTMENT

For a lot of people it would be a great experience to sit in Stanford Stadium amidst a crowd of 78,265 fans cheering the USA's first Olympic victory in 60 years. As much as I enjoyed that 3-0 win in 1984 over Costa Rica, it was also one of the most difficult days of my life. I'd been cut from the squad only two weeks before.

The circumstances leading up to my being cut made it even tougher to swallow. Along with several of my peers, I had taken two

Fig. 9.5. Before I made it to the demanding world of German football, I had my character tested by an Olympic-sized disappointment. I know now that if I had reacted immaturely, I would probably not have experienced the thrills I've enjoyed since then.

quarters away from college to tour with what we expected would become the USA's Olympic Team. For approximately eight months we trained under then National Team coach, Alkis Panagoulias. The idea of participating in an Olympics was doubly exciting for me, as we were scheduled to play all of our first-round matches in my home state.

Only a few weeks prior to the Games, it was announced that pros who hadn't appeared in a World Cup would be deemed eligible. Just like that, almost all of us were given our walking papers in favor of North American Soccer League veterans.

I suffered a double whammy. NCAA rules state that one must earn a minimum number of academic units per year to play the following

Respect all coaching and refereeing decisions.

semester. That stipulation can be waived under a handful of circumstances, Olympic participation being one. But since I'd been cut, I no longer qualified for the waiver!

It wasn't that I'd been cut that got me the most upset. What really bothered me was that I wasn't given the opportunity to play with or against the pros. Over half a year of hard work and dedication was rendered meaningless through no fault of our own. And, no, I didn't think it was fair. But, regardless of my own personal sentiments, I also realized that it wasn't up to me to name the squad. That's the responsibility of the coaching staff.

I knew that there are times as an athlete when it's best not to say how you're feeling. My dad had taught me years before that players must respect coaching decisions, even when those decisions directly affected you in an adverse way. I'm grateful for that advice. I went to every game and supported my country's team. It was hard to get past my own ego, but doing so made me feel better about myself. I feel that, in my own very small way, I contributed something to the team.

That experience helped me to relate to how Frank Klopas must have felt during the 1994 World Cup. After showing incredible determination to rehabilitate a serious knee injury in order to play in pre-Cup exhibition matches, he went on a scoring binge that earned him a place on our 22-man roster. Despite his hot streak, he didn't see any action during the Cup. And he handled it like the great pro that he is.

Only later did I learn that Frank had been told by Bora that he would play against Romania. In that game we needed but a draw to win our group, which would have meant getting to face a demoralized Argentina team (without the suspended Diego Maradona) instead of champions-to-be Brazil in the round of 16.

We fell behind Romania early, 1-0, and that's how the score remained. On our bench sat a bona fide goal scorer who had to feel that he had a contribution to make if only he'd be given the chance. Nevertheless, Frank never complained to anyone. By placing the team above his personal needs, he enhanced his own reputation as a class act and contributed to the sense of unity that was a key factor in our success.

At some point in your career your character will be tested. After having started all three USA games of Italia '90, I came home from Germany in 1992 to be fully available to Bora. Even though it was quite a financial sacrifice to come home, I did so because that would give me a far better chance of playing in the first World Cup to be held on American soil.

Things went well at first until I was inexplicably left behind on back-to-back road trips. My name wasn't included on the roster for the 1993 CONCACAF Gold Cup. My disappointment was compounded by the confusion of not knowing if Bora was testing me, if he wasn't happy with my form, or if he was sending a message to the entire team that nobody should take his job for granted.

While the team competed, my wife, Dawn, and I vacationed in Hawaii. I did a lot of soul searching. The more I evaluated my own attitude, work ethic, and how I thought I'd been playing, the less sense I could make of having been dropped.

It was during that hiatus that I had opportunities to sign with teams in Germany and England. Tempting as that was, I recalled my dad's advice when I wanted to quit youth football—always see all your commitments through. I went to train with England's Charlton Athletic to remain fit during the Gold Cup. So that there could be no misunderstanding, I made it clear to them that I planned on rejoining the U.S. team in our Mission Viejo, California, camp.

The only constructive approach that I could take was to redouble my determination to give 100 percent effort in every U.S. practice and, when given another chance, to play so well in every game that there was no question that I'd done my best. Doing so would improve the odds that I'd be selected, but nothing in sports is guaranteed. Still, even if I failed to make the team, I would have the peace of mind of knowing that I'd done the best that I could.

In the interim I was very careful to measure my words when speaking with teammates and the media. When I next saw Bora I didn't challenge his authority by asking, "How come I didn't play?" Instead, I asked him what I could do to improve.

As a player, you should never be timid about approaching your coach with an honest concern, provided that you express yourself constructively and at the appropriate time and place. For instance, game days aren't recommended for such conversations. Instead, ask your coach after a practice when he or she might have a few free minutes to chat.

I can't pretend that I wasn't angry and hurt. Having contributed a lot to a succession of USA squads for several years, I felt I deserved better. Looking back at that incident now, I'm glad I handled it well. If not, I doubt I would have started all four of the USA's games in the 1994 Cup.

I'm sure you've heard the cliché about turning a negative into a positive. The essence of being an athlete is to understand that you'll face challenges throughout your career. Losers find excuses for failures. Winners seek solutions to problems.

PUTTING THE *WE* AHEAD OF THE *ME*

Two of the greatest moments in my career—the victory over Trinidad that got us to Italy and UCLA's winning the 1985 NCAA Division I national championship—were marked by great unselfishness by a teammate.

The "other" Andy Burke was named John Stollmeyer. A hardworking defensive midfielder, John made a great contribution to our qualifying run leading up to the 1990 World Cup. The decisive game was in the jam-packed National Stadium in Port of Spain, Trinidad.

If ever a citizenry rallied around a team as a symbol, it was with that Trinidad squad. Their nation was just beginning to recover from a severe economic depression, and the successes of their soccer squad became a national metaphor. Such was the fervor generated by their team that the Trinidad government had already declared the day after the match a national holiday!

Nor did our side lack a sense of purpose. The late astronaut Sonny Carter was scheduled that day to fly the space shuttle. Before that mission he taped an inspirational message to our team. And, with the U.S. already named as the host nation of the following World Cup, we knew that getting to Italy would help us be far more competitive in 1994.

Although we were tied in the standings (with nine points apiece), Trinidad enjoyed a superior goal differential. A draw meant they would advance. We had to win the game.

John Stollmeyer was my roommate for that trip. As much as being named to start meant to me, it would have meant even more to John. His family had come to America from Trinidad, and he still had relatives living down there. In fact, Stollmeyer Castle remains a major tourist attraction to this day.

While John had started all but one of our qualifying games, I was coming off a stress fracture to my foot that had put me out of commission for two months. Nevertheless, the day before the match,

Fig. 9.6. Always a class act, Desmond Armstrong shows his great team spirit in the days just before one of the most important matches in U.S. soccer history.

Coach Bob Gansler announced that I would be our defensive midfielder instead of John. I was given the number 15 shirt that normally belonged to defender Desmond Armstrong. It was to be the only time in my soccer career that I wore that number.

Rarely have athletes handled such a keen disappointment with more class than did John and Desmond. Not once did they let their feelings show. They couldn't have been any more supportive of me. Because of their great character, we avoided what could have been an awkward situation that might have diverted my focus.

The story certainly had a happy ending. My role was to nullify Trinidad's midfield maestro, Russell Latapy. I knew that I would have my hands full, as he is both a gifted and experienced player. He was certainly their key man.

Given my assignment and that our team had managed to produce but five goals in our seven previous qualifying matches, I was about as probable a candidate to find the scoresheet as Andy Burke.

We got a huge break early-on when John Doyle threw a cross-body block to bring down Philbert Jones in our box. Luckily, no penalty kick was awarded. In the 31st minute John Harkes was on the wrong end of a crunching tackle. The ball and John went flying in opposite directions (he went down, the ball went over the sideline). Tab Ramos quickly threw the ball in to Brian Bliss, who returned it to Tab.

I was standing toward the middle of the field, trying to look as nonchalant as possible in the hope that their defenders would overlook me. Seeing me open and square to the play, Tab flicked a pass in my direction. I received the bouncing ball somewhat awkwardly with a combination of a chest/stomach trap that redirected it toward their goal. As I ran forward, a defender raced out to meet me. I faked a shot with my right foot. My defender made the mistake of jumping at me, which allowed me to cut the ball across my body and toward my left foot.

Looking up, I realized that I was approaching the very outer edge of shooting range. I didn't hesitate. I knew that from over 30 yards away that I would need a combination of power, accuracy, and topspin if I was to beat their goalie, Michael Maurice. Once that volley left my foot I knew it would be on target and that it had a chance to be dangerous. Somehow, the ball sailed just inches beyond Maurice's outstretched fingertips. What had been a carnival atmosphere turned into instant and almost complete silence. Only the shouts of my teammates were audible.

When we left the locker room after halftime, our attitude was complete determination. We were convinced there was no way we would let that lead slip away. For the remainder of that afternoon, John Harkes worked like a mule, Tony Meola made some key saves, and Tab Ramos danced on the ball to keep possession. Every one of my teammates rose to the occasion to produce what remains, in my opinion, the turning point for U.S. soccer.

Being the last of the 24 teams to qualify for the World Cup was no small feat for a nation that had last participated in that event 40 years earlier. I will also always remember the way that the Trinidad players handled losing. Their players wished us good luck. Jack Warner, who later became the president of CONCACAF but who was the president of their federation at that time, told us to represent our country just as they would have represented theirs. Fans, many with tears still in their eyes, came up to shake our hands.

I know it was my goal that got the headlines, but I was no more responsible for the victory than was Tony, John, Tab, or, for that matter, Desmond Armstrong and John Stollmeyer.

You can learn a lot from the examples set by Andy Burke, Desmond, and John. The only things that you'll "accomplish" by taking the low road are to make yourself look petty and selfish while hurting your team. The class shown by that trio was rewarded: Burke won a national title and Stollmeyer and Armstrong got to play in the 1990 World Cup.

BELIEVING IN YOUR ABILITIES

Just as cockiness is inappropriate so, too, is being overawed at a situation. Being confident is every bit as important to your success as having the requisite skill and athleticism.

The most intimidating of circumstances I've ever found myself in came toward the end of my career at UCLA. Sigi called me into his office one afternoon to inform me that I had been selected as the only American representative to play in the upcoming FIFA World All-Star Game at the Rose Bowl. Of course, I thought he was joking.

Believe me, it's quite a jump from college soccer to sharing a locker room with Diego Maradona and a host of Brazilian superstars. Naturally, I wasn't in the starting lineup. It was well into the second half when I was told to warm up, with our team trailing, 2-0.

With about 20 minutes remaining I jogged onto a field that was inhabited by a who's who of the sport. I was enough of a realist to know that they all had far more experience than me. But I also knew that I had a job to do, and I couldn't be intimidated by the circumstances. I made up my mind to play just as I always had.

My first test came when facing a two-on-one. I was the one. The two consisted of West German star Felix Magath and Denmark's ball wizard, Jasper Olsen. Olsen took a rocket of a shot. I stuck out my foot. The ball hit it so hard that my leg went numb. The tingling sensation lasted for several minutes.

Our team came back to tie the game before winning it in a penalty kick shootout. I played a minor role in the build-up that led to our first goal. On the subsequent equalizer, I booted a 50-yard cross-field diagonal pass to Roberto Cabanas, who got the ball to Maradona. Diego did the rest.

That game turned out to be my big break. Magath was about to retire to a management position with Hamburg, which traditionally had been one of the most prestigious clubs in the West German Bundesliga. He made it known to me that he was quite interested in giving me a shot with their team.

That night I had the thrill of having dinner with the incomparable Franz Beckenbauer. He advised me to seek a higher level of competition in order to become the best player I could be.

As I look back at that game, I realize that I had good sense just to play it as if it were UCLA-Santa Clara. I didn't try to show off by doing things I couldn't do. Nor was I so intimidated that I treated the ball like a hot potato.

If there's one attribute that American athletes seem to possess in abundance, it's confidence. I know many sports figures in Germany who greatly admire us for our "can do" attitude. As long as you believe in yourself, you should do well. But never let your confidence cross the line to become arrogance.

DEALING WITH COACHES

Many young athletes don't respond well to criticism. We'd all rather be complimented. No matter how harsh words might seem, remember that your coach's job is to help you and the team to perform your best. Even if you don't agree with everything that's said, you should try to maintain an open mind and show respect.

I've been fortunate in that I've played for a succession of coaches who had a lot to offer. Many players aren't that lucky. Soccer is still relatively new in our country. There remains a high ratio of participants to experienced coaches who once played the game themselves. It isn't that unusual to have players thinking that they know more about the sport than does their coach. And, in many cases, they're right.

If you find yourself in such a situation it's important that you show your coach the respect that he or she deserves. Always remember that if not for that person's willingness to give of his or her time you wouldn't have a team.

Also, have an open mind. You'd be surprised how much you can learn from any person with experience in athletics even if that experience wasn't soccer-related. But you'll only learn if you are receptive to that person's comments.

The more respectful you are to him or her, the more receptive that coach is likely to be when you present a constructive idea. Ask your coach if he or she can set aside some time. At that meeting you might say something to the effect of, "One of my former coaches had a great shooting drill. May I show it to you?" Make certain that this is said in one-on-one conversation. This will avoid that coach feeling that his or her authority is being threatened.

One other point: no matter how substantial are your coach's credentials there will likely be some decisions that you will struggle to understand. I'm still not certain why Bora decided to omit me from the USA's CONCACAF Gold Cup roster. I just have to assume that any coach who had already done well in two World Cups must have a valid reason for any action that he took and that it wasn't my place to call into question any of his decisions.

CONDUCTING YOURSELF OFF THE FIELD

One of the greatest pieces of advice my dad gave me was that "you've got to give up something to get something." Becoming a top-class athlete requires sacrifice. There are times when others are partying that you must be in bed. You must treat your body with respect and not put anything harmful into it, like drugs or alcohol. You need to keep a healthy diet.

You have to give up something to get something.

—*Robert Caligiuri*

Are there world-class athletes who have abused themselves? Unfortunately, yes. But I dare say that doing so limited their effectiveness. How great could Diego Maradona or George Best have been had they possessed the discipline of Franz Beckenbauer?

I'm sure you've heard about players with great talent whose poor (and well-publicized) life choices greatly harmed or ended their professional careers. Invariably, athletes and the teams they play for must pay a price for indiscretion and irresponsibility. Let me state this unequivocally: I don't use illegal drugs. I don't smoke cigarettes. I don't abuse alcohol. And I never will. I've got too much at stake. I also make every effort to watch my diet, knowing that good nutrition is important to performing my best. I get adequate sleep, and I stay in shape during the off-season.

I wish you could observe how the members of the U.S. National Team conduct ourselves on the road. We are very much aware that we're representing ourselves, our families, our sport, and our nation. If you come to our team hotel during the days before a match, you won't see any of us frolicking in the pool or hanging out in the bar until the wee hours of the morning. We know our purpose. We understand that we are expected to perform at our best during every training session. If we're lucky, our bodies will hold up long enough for us play professional soccer until we're in our mid- to late-30s. There will be ample time after that to stay up late or go swimming. Until then, we'll save our energy for where it is really needed—on the field.

The older you get, and the more high-profile you become, the greater will be the temptations to sway you from what you know is right. You'll have to make choices that weigh instant gratification against long-term gain. Being mature and responsible pays dividends in the end.

Your responsibilities as a college player include committing to academic excellence. This means you must budget your time to reflect your priorities. If getting your homework done means missing a social gathering you'd really like to attend, then so be it—you miss the gathering. Sure, there will be times when you just won't feel like making the necessary sacrifices. There's nothing wrong with feeling that way, but this doesn't mean you should succumb to such feelings. I got through them, and you can too. Recall the great motto of the Civil Rights movement: Keep your eyes on the prize. If necessary, take a minute to daydream about just how great it will feel when you finally do realize your goals. Let the inspiration of such thoughts be the fuel to keep you going.

Fig. 9.7. Romario could not have become the great player he is without spending countless hours on his own, honing his ball skills.

Were there times when I almost gave in to circumstances? You bet! I can still vividly recall practicing as a teenager in Germany with my eyebrows frozen. Nor was I always thrilled to be running on my own in the blistering summer heat of southern California in preparation for a Junior National Team Camp, while the rest of my high school buddies were hangin' on the beach. It wasn't a lot of fun experiencing the pre-World Cup soccer saturation featuring Bora's two-a-day sessions, where our "breaks" consisted of team meals and watching match tapes together.

Yes, I was sometimes tempted to skip a grueling training session or an independent workout and go have fun with my friends. But looking back now on the sacrifices I had to make, they add an extra sense of pride to everything that I've accomplished in soccer. Even if I never played one minute in one pro game, I'd know the great self-satisfaction of having become the best I could be.

FINAL THOUGHTS

Make it a point after every match to utter two of the most important words in our language: Thank you. Thank your coach. Thank the referee. Thank your teammates. And thank your parents for all of the many times they've driven you to games, all of the fund-raisers they engaged in for your team's benefit, and for just being 100% behind you all the way.

I certainly know the debt of gratitude that I owe to my dad, my wife, my coaches, and my teammates. And I also owe a huge thank you to the dedication of soccer administrators like the USSF's Alan Rothenberg and Hank Steinbrecher, whose expertise and incredible work ethic resulted in America putting on the greatest World Cup in history (which, in turn, paved the way for the launching of Major League Soccer so that you and your friends can share my childhood dream of playing top-class professional soccer in your native land).

As you continue to progress in the sport, you'll be judged by your first touch, your ability to get behind an opponent with a great move, and the coolness with which you slot the ball past their keeper and into the net. But you'll also be assessed by your commitment and your

© Jon Van Woerden

Fig. 9.10. All of us in U.S. soccer owe a debt of gratitude to the likes of Alan Rothenberg (right), seen here with the legendary Dutch coach, Rinus Michels.

© Jon Van Woerden

Fig. 9.11. Players like Tab aren't born winners—they get there through dedication and perseverance.

character. It's in the hard times when your team isn't doing well that you'll show the type of person that you are.

Test yourself on how many of the following terms apply to you: dedication, unselfishness, perseverance, respectfulness, high moral standards, sportsmanship, class, competitiveness. Being a winner involves much more than merely outscoring an opponent. And you're never a loser if your team comes up short, as long as you've given your best.

The most respected athletes are the ones who combine greatness during competition with great class. That's why the likes of Pele, Jackie Robinson, Larry Bird, Wayne Gretzky, Billie Jean King, Mario Lemieux, Muhammad Ali, Franz Beckenbauer, Jack Nicklaus, Arthur Ashe, Michael Jordan, and so many others live on long after their careers have ended or are winding down.

Your actions and words are always being judged. Win or lose, you must conduct yourself in a way that brings honor to yourself, your family, your team, and, when applicable, to your club, school, state, or country.

CHAPTER

10

Setting Your Sights on the Next Level

*"**B**e global in your self-appraisal."*

College soccer improves every year. The number of good players, the level of coaching, and the quality of the facilities are all moving in the right direction. College soccer can be the bridge between youth sports and turning pro. At its best, it's a fantastic experience.

Starting college is a period in your life when you'll experience new responsibilities. Foremost of these will be learning how to budget your time between academic demands, your athletic schedule, and social concerns. The pressures placed on you can be stressful, but with the right priorities and guidance, you should persevere. Having done so, you'll leave campus an adult.

Getting to the school of your choice involves many factors, not the least of which requires you to take several steps well in advance to improve your marketability. I'll discuss these considerations in detail in the hope of improving your odds of playing for the school of your choice.

First, however, some words on one of your biggest life decisions. Selecting which school to attend is like entering into a four-year marriage. The compatibility of the partners (the school, the soccer program, and yourself) is the essential factor.

A soccer player's beauty is in the eye of the beholder. A coach who plays a direct style will likely be looking for size, speed, and strength, whereas a coach whose team builds from the back will place a greater premium on skill and smarts, even if that means sacrificing physical attributes. By watching a team play, you'll come to appreciate a given coach's vision of the game. And this will give you a clue as to whether you're well-suited for that school's playing style.

However—and this is important—on most teams, there is a place or two reserved for the proverbial square peg in the round hole. For instance, as skillful as the 1994 Brazilians were, the ball-winning attributes of the very physical Dunga in the midfield were every bit as important to their success as their overall mastery of the ball. As another example, Wimbledon, which tends to be the most direct club in the English League, always includes a playmaker in their lineup.

Before setting your sights on playing for a specific school (or even narrowing the field to a few candidates), honestly appraise your abilities and that team's needs. Only if there's a fit is it worth your while to pursue that avenue. If you're a goalie as a high school senior, it doesn't make much sense to sign with a college whose freshman keeper plays like Kasey Keller.

Learn the coach's style and demands. Do you want to play for a strict disciplinarian who will do everything in his or her power to make you a better player, or are you looking for someone who pals around with the team after games?

You must also know yourself. Is your real goal to be an All-American? Is it to play professional soccer? Or is it to make a contribution to the team? Perhaps you'll be happy just to be a part of the program.

You may be content to ride the bench for two years if you feel you're improving by training against better players. That way when you do hit the field, you'll be more ready to compete than if you'd been thrown to the wolves by first playing as a freshman. On the other hand, you might thrive on challenge and feel ready to handle the physical and psychological demands of playing right away. Perhaps you want instant gratification. If your ego demands to play immediately, I wouldn't recommend going the Atlantic Coast Conference route unless you're really a strong and stable player. Also, the institution you pick must fit your academic and social needs. It's shortsighted to attend college assuming that your time there will be only a stepping stone to a professional athletic career.

If your goal is to become a pro, that's great. But make sure to walk the athletic high wire with the academic safety net of a good education to protect against any falls (including, but not limited to, a career-ending injury). Always strive to excel academically as well as athletically. The well-educated athlete has the edge of being able to cope in corporate America. In my case, that has helped me secure some valuable endorsements and, of equal importance, I'll have some doors open when my playing days are done. Even in Europe, where soccer players earn the highest salaries, only a few top stars can afford not to work after retiring from the game.

Give considerable thought about how you're going to decide which school best suits your needs, as well as what to do to earn admission and perhaps get financial aid.

BE REALISTIC

As you move toward college soccer, step one is to be realistic. It's human nature to enjoy being complimented, but view positive publicity like poison: It only hurts if you swallow it. Too many young players tend to hear just the good things about themselves. Don't read your own headlines and think that you're all-world just because you have been able to dominate in your small domain. That won't impress anybody at the next level. There's no great honor in being all-block on a dead-end street!

You need to be global in your self-appraisal. Don't judge yourself by how you've done at the level at which you're competing today. Instead, assess yourself by how you'd be able to fare at the highest level of soccer to which you aspire to play.

While you should be realistic and somewhat self-critical to identify the aspects of your game that most need improvement, you shouldn't lack self-confidence. You'll go far if you believe in yourself and do your best to outwork others.

I strongly suggest that if your aspirations include playing intercollegiate soccer that by the start of your sophomore year of high school you seek out respected college coaches to gain their feedback on what aspects of your game require the most attention. A great avenue is to

Fig. 10.1.   To get to this level you must be global and realistic in your self-appraisal.

attend one of the many summer soccer camps that are staffed by college coaches (it's especially useful if the camp runs the gamut from the Division I to Division III levels). Check out the camp in advance by talking to those who have previously attended to make sure that it's all that it claims to be. Such camps aren't inexpensive. I washed a lot of cars and mowed more lawns than I care to remember to help pay my way. The hard work was worth it.

One of the many legacies of the U.S. having hosted the 1994 World Cup and of Major League Soccer's existence is that your generation has been exposed to top-level soccer. By watching matches of that caliber you have gained insight about the qualities required to be a bona fide player. An added plus of MLS is that there are role models/soccer heroes that you can seek to emulate. With very rare exception, those playing pro soccer in America are nice people. Don't be shy about writing one of them to ask for advice. This also goes for the members of our Women's National Team or your favorite college player. You may be pleasantly surprised at just how responsive and helpful soccer players tend to be.

PLAY WITH STYLE

The athletes who made up the rosters of the University of Virginia teams of the early- and mid-1990s may be the best domestic models of what's needed to play what's known as total football. It's a style in which all players are capable of attacking effectively when their team is on offense, and all are competent defenders when the opponents have the ball.

Generally speaking, those Cavs were smart players. They were very athletic. They handled themselves on the field well and were technically solid. They were well coached. They didn't have any glaring weaknesses that their opponents could hope to exploit. And they were versatile. The 1994 Virginia team entered the NCAA Final minus their ace playmaker, Mike Fisher, owing to an accumulation of yellow cards. And even the talented Fisher would have been Coach Bruce Arena's second choice that season had Claudio Reyna not left school a year early to begin his professional career in Germany.

UVA's tactics in that final against a strong Indiana University squad were very different from the wide-open approach they had used in winning their semifinal match two days earlier and which had become their trademark as they were on the brink of claiming their fifth NCAA Division I championship in six seasons. Putting enormous pressure on whichever IU player had the ball, they suffocated and frustrated a Hoosier midfield that featured Todd Yeagley and Brian Maisonneuve.

Only because each of the Cavs players was versatile could the team so dramatically alter its strategy on such short notice. That, in a nutshell, is what the coaches often look for in the German Bundesliga. The men that I have played with and against are almost all technically sound, tactically aware, athletically gifted, fully fit, and totally committed to striving for excellence. This well-rounded approach is why the Germans have had such fantastic success internationally, having reached five of the seven World Cup Finals (winning two of them) from 1966 through 1990.

Back in his coaching days, my friend from Reebok, Don Rawson, would play a training game he called Find the Dork. He asked his athletes to determine which of their opponents wasn't as gifted as the other players on the field. Whenever that player received the ball, he would be placed under immediate pressure.

That strategy also works at the higher levels of the sport. In the 1994 World Cup, Brazil was superb at reading the situations in which pressure could result in a turnover. Years before, the Germans introduced what many observers called the web. Like a spider's trap, they showed a false space to entice opponents into positions in which offensive options would be limited. Once that trap had been set, the defender nearest the attacker in possession forced that foe toward a covering defender.

The more versatile you are, the less likely a foe will be able to play to any specific weakness. Don't underestimate the value of being an all-around player—both to your team and to improving your chances of maintaining a place in the lineup.

The defining moments of my career occurred in different positions. I was a defensive midfielder in the game against Trinidad and Tobago when I scored the goal that helped to get us into the 1990 World Cup. My goal in the Cup against the Czechs came while I was being used on the right side in the back.

I was a left fullback four years later, when we shocked the world with our 2-1 upset of Colombia in the Rose Bowl. In fact, had it not been for my strong left foot that allowed me to play on the left side, it's doubtful if I would even have made the USA's 1994 roster. For that, I can thank all of those hours that I spent as a youngster working on my "other" foot against the garage door of our house.

© Jon Van Woerden

Fig. 10.2. On this day in Trinidad I was a defensive midfielder lucky enough to produce the best attacking moment of my career. It wouldn't have been possible if I hadn't had the versatility for Coach Bob Gansler to play me in an unfamiliar role.

The 3-0 upset of Argentina in the 1995 Copa America was doubly meaningful to me, as I became only the 26th player in history to earn his 100th cap. In that game I was switched to sweeper in the 16th minute when Marcelo Balboa departed with an injury.

Years before that, I had helped Walnut High School in Walnut, California, capture four league titles as a striker. It was at UCLA that Coach Sigi Schmid moved me into a central defender's role, which is where I played when we won the 1985 NCAA Division I national title.

If not for my versatility, it's unlikely that I'd have lasted nearly as long as I have. Consider this to rank among the best tips I'll offer—

the more roles you can fill for your team, the more you'll achieve in the sport.

After Sheffield Wednesday lost an international defender due to an injury, the coach called upon midfielder John Harkes to play in the back. That was John's big break in English football. Thomas Dooley is equally valuable to our National Team as a defensive midfielder or as a sweeper. Roy Wegerle can play in several roles, as can Mike Sorber. When we needed a fullback, Steve Sampson converted Mike Burns, and Mike has performed as if he'd played as a defender all his life. Jeff Agoos has played as a left midfielder and left fullback for the National Team and performs as a sweeper for DC United.

Versatile players are rare because precious few coaches think about an athlete's future beyond that team. Most coaches see their mandate as finding a way to win with the talent at their disposal. They place each player in a role in which his or her strengths are maximized and weaknesses minimized.

For instance, left-footed folks usually play on the left side, where they are rarely required to use their right foot. That's fine for the short-term needs of that squad and to help that coach remain employed, but if you're that left-footed player you should actively seek out opportunities in formal practices and on your own to use your right foot in matchlike situations. Through repetition, you'll improve those areas of your game that now represent the weakest spot in your armor.

If your coach is approachable, mention that you were told by your summer camp coach or advised by college coaches to work on certain things. If it helps, tell him that Paul Caligiuri made the suggestion. Request that your coach help you upgrade those areas in training. If that doesn't mesh with your coach's needs (keeping in mind that the coach has limited time in which to put a finished product on the field), ask if you can work together after the formal portion of the practice session.

Constantly challenge yourself. If you're a forward, find the best defender on your team. The two of you should go at it as often as possible, whenever a drill or a training game requires defenders to work against attackers. Aside from satisfying a short-term ego problem, there's nothing to be gained by constantly beating the weak link in your team's defense. Play to your strength in a game, but work on your weaknesses in practice. Make a concerted effort during training to use your so-called chocolate foot (the one that tends to melt when the heat is on).

Of equal importance, don't waste opportunities to improve in matches in which the score isn't close. This is the time to continue to work hard, as you are constantly competing with opponents, team-mates, and, above all, yourself. If your team is up or down by several goals, you can either relax, or you can have the maturity to view this as a chance to constructively experiment in a game environment by trying that new move you've been working on in practice.

The University of North Carolina dominated women's college soccer throughout the 1980s and well into the 1990s. Coach Anson Dorrance would often give his players restrictions once it was clear that his team would win that match. For example, he might tell them that they had to play two-touch, with the expectation that they must score twice within the next 20 minutes. Having a goal is important in maintaining a competitive environment.

SHOULD YOU PLAY UP?

You must also be willing to put yourself in an environment in which you're no longer the star. I don't advocate playing up to the point of being overwhelmed. There's no use competing against kids who are so vastly superior that you never get to touch the ball or, when you do, you lose it every time. But you should play at the best level of competition at which you can hold your head above water. Todd Yeagley's winning the 1994 Missouri Athletic Club Sports Foundation's Collegiate Soccer Player of the Year Award was aided by his chance to play at summer camp as a teenager against veteran Indiana University standouts. There were times that he got the stuffing beat out of him, but he was psychologically tough, and the experience made him better. So, too, with Jovan Kirovski, currently one of the most exciting talents on the U.S. soccer scene. Long before he left for European professional football as a 16-year old, he played in Sunday morning pick-up games with and against adults. Like Todd and Jovan, try to put yourself in environments that make you react faster, both technically and tactically.

LET'S GET SERIOUS

Although it's never too late to dedicate yourself to achieving a goal, the longer you wait before becoming a serious player, the more priceless time you will have squandered. When you began playing at a competitive level, you were making the statement, "Soccer is my sport and I'm serious about becoming good at it."

Take a look at how many hours serious athletes practice in the individual sports where it's them against a clock or a single rival. I can guarantee you that there are countless kids growing up in the traditional, powerful soccer nations to whom playing this sport represents an unbridled passion. Their soccer ball accompanies them virtually everywhere they go.

There will be times when you can fool parents, coaches, teammates, and referees. But you'll never fool the ball. It's vital to practice your skills on a daily basis. If you don't spend enough hours with that ball, you'll never develop skill on demand. And, without that, you'll always be limited as a player.

© Wilfried Witters/Hamburg

Fig. 10.3. If you're a serious player, you practice any time and anywhere you can.

What does all of this have to do with selecting the right college to attend? My answer is that your options will be only as limitless as your game. If you have a glaring weakness or two, you're far less likely to be judged as suitable for any of the finer Division I programs.

Your versatility is increasingly crucial with each step you progress up the soccer ladder. You can dominate most high school games by relying on one outstanding attribute. Superb athletes can use speed and jumping ability to score dozens of goals despite weak fundamental skills. Sadly, the majority of very fast youngsters never develop the wide array of ball skills they need to later compete successfully against opponents who are just as fast as they are.

I'm a firm believer that competition is a great coach and one of your best vehicles toward improving. Seeking out the most challenging environment you're capable of competing in is an important step. To dominate kids your own age either through superior athleticism or talent (or both) can lead to bad habits. There's nothing wrong with being a star on your school team, but augment that experience by actively seeking out competition in which you're a small fish in a bigger pond. I was only 16 when I first played for South Bay United's Under-23 team, which was comprised primarily of college players.

Competition is the best coach.

—Hank Steinbrecher

It's amazing how many superior athletes who are all-state strikers in high school end up as fullbacks in college (where their physical qualities are useful mainly to negate athletic opponents who do have skill). And many of those all-state types find themselves unable to compete even in that role, which relegates them to a spot on the bench or to "stardom" on an intramural team.

Soccer often breaks down to a series of one-on-one battles all over the field. The more versatile your skills, the more of those battles you'll win. The more of those battles you win, the more valuable you'll be to your team. And the more valuable you are to your team, the more options you'll have.

FOUR KEYS TO SUCCESS

Different coaches value different qualities when judging candidates. But let's start with the premise that there are four basic components to the modern game: technical, tactical, physical, and psychological.

1. *Technical*

Being "technical" is just a fancy term made up in coaching schools—all it really means is being skillful. Don't fool yourself into assuming that because you can juggle a ball a few zillion times and have mastered a half dozen dribbling tricks that you're now a skillful player. To have skill is to be able to produce whatever ball touch is needed when under pressure from an opponent in limited space. If you're playing abroad where the game tends to be more physical, you had better be able to consistently produce that skill while some monster is breathing (or worse) down your neck. And you must be able to do it when conditions aren't conducive to your game, such as on a muddy field while the rain is pelting down and the wind is howling. Skill is useful only if it's effective when your comfort zone has been tweaked. There are players who aren't technically proficient but who somehow make things happen in match situations.

There's a story I heard in Germany about Berti Vogts. You may know him as the man who followed Franz Beckenbauer as the coach of Germany's National Team. He was also Franz's teammate on the side that defeated Holland, 2-1, to win the 1974 World Cup.

The legend goes that in the locker room after that Final, Vogts kissed the Cup. He then dropped to his knees and declared, "I'm a world champion, and I can't even juggle a ball five times!"

I can't vouch for whether that tale is fact or myth, but I can attest to playing with athletes who weren't naturally gifted but who found a way to get the job done when it mattered. And I've seen others that are all-world in practice but who can't reproduce that form in a match. Vogts wasn't elegant on the ball, but he knew not to attempt things he couldn't do. By playing to his strengths, using his intelligence, and through the pure strength of his will to prevail, he became a world champion. However, while it's true that possessing one or two exceptional attributes can camouflage a weakness, it's

© Jon Van Woerden

Fig. 10.4. San Jose Clash star forward Eric Wynalda has the ability to apply his skills at high speed and under pressure from opponents.

also true that the more well-rounded you can become, the better off you'll be.

As you work on becoming well-rounded, make certain that your first touch is among your strongest suits. If your first touch is poor, it may be your last touch! A good first touch is common to all great players. The greatest of the great have a first touch that either gets them out of difficulty or places the opposition in trouble. It buys you that vital extra yard or two that allows you more time and space to do something positive on subsequent touches.

2. *Tactical*

Tactics are the decisions that involve how you apply your skill. How many times have you seen shooters blast the ball over the bar from close range when accuracy, not power, was called for? In all situations, assess your options before receiving the ball in order to select the choice that will best help your team. This also requires an understanding of how, when, and where to move off the ball.

3. *Physical*

All the skill in the world and the intelligence to apply it won't amount to a hill of beans if you're too slow to get open. While it's true that not every world-class soccer star possesses world-class speed, you do need a certain amount of pace, strength, agility, balance, and leaping ability to be able to compete successfully.

Just how important the physical parameters are to top-level soccer was underscored to me when I joined St. Pauli of the German Bundesliga in 1995. Nearly every week a former decathlon star put us through an entire training session designed to improve our running techniques. Included were several drills that saw us hopping, backpedaling, and running sideways. Even though I was 31 at that time, I found I was able to improve my movements.

4. *Psychological*

You've undoubtedly heard it said that the difference between winning and losing in the pros is often mental. The true measure of an athlete is how he or she reacts to adversity.

The world is full of "blue sky players" who excel when everything is going their way (Sigi Schmid calls them "dancers" because "when the floor gets sticky, they don't want to know"). But how do you perform when you're in the middle of a losing streak, when top teammates are sidelined with injuries, when the field is sloppy, when that bully marking you is allowed to get away with murder by an overly lenient referee, when your team is down two goals, or when the fans on the road are questioning the circumstances of your birth? When it comes to mental toughness, I have developed a great admiration for German soccer. Their qualities are epitomized by their number one sporting hero, Franz Beckenbauer.

In 1966 Beckenbauer's team lost a heartbreaking 4-2 extra time match to the hosting English. Replays confirm that the go-ahead goal

Fig. 10.5. The fierce competitiveness and determination of Michelle Akers were key ingredients in helping the USA capture the 1991 Women's World Championship.

should never have counted. Geoff Hurst's shot hit the underside of the crossbar, bounced on the goal line, and returned to the field of play. It's likely that England would not have won without that score, as their next goal came in the dying moments of the game on a breakaway after West Germany had pushed virtually their entire team forward in an attempt to net an equalizer. Ever the sportsman, Beckenbauer handled that decision with pure class. He didn't vigorously protest the goal at the time or blame the referee for his team's loss.

Four years later, Franz suffered another great disappointment in a World Cup. The 4-3 semifinal loss to Italy (once again in extra time) might have been reversed with a fully fit Beckenbauer. He was fouled badly from behind just before he could dribble into the Italian penalty area. Falling awkwardly, Franz dislocated his shoulder and was forced to play the remainder of the match in excruciating pain with his arm taped to his side. Once again, Beckenbauer offered no excuses; nor did his determination to prevail ever falter. If anything, he used those two bitter disappointments as a source of motivation. His was a classic case of how a player can turn a negative into a positive.

Franz's reward came in 1974 at a packed Olympic Stadium in front of a partisan crowd of 77,833. The 2-1 upset of Johan Cruyff's great Dutch team allowed Captain Beckenbauer to lift the most coveted trophy in international sports.

I have often thought about the qualities that made Franz one of the greatest players our game will ever know. As much as I admire his vision, skills, and his incredible understanding of the sport, I am an even bigger fan of his attitude. In times of personal crisis, I sometimes ask myself how Franz would handle a similar situation.

THE BOTTOM LINE

I've given you a laundry list of qualities that I think you will need to get to the next level. To sum up:

- Can you make the ball do what you want with either foot (and with all the other appropriate body parts)?
- Can you pick out the appropriate skill for every situation?
- Can you consistently beat an opponent to 50-50 balls for 90 minutes?
- Can you handle the stresses of the game?

If your answers to these four questions are "yes, yes, yes, and yes," then you're the genuine item. But if you're the genuine item, I can guarantee you didn't answer "yes, yes, yes, and yes," because truly outstanding players are *never* satisfied with their game. They always strive to improve.

Most college coaches will evaluate candidates based on the four factors I've just listed. You have the makings of being a solid role player if you're above average in one area and competent in the other three. Being outstanding in one area and above average in the others could make you one of a college team's key players. Being well above average in all four could be your ticket to advancing to the next level beyond college.

You'll be evaluated by most college coaches and their scouts based on where you currently stand in these categories and where they project your potential may lie. Don't be surprised if that coach/scout does a lot of homework. Unlike in football or basketball programs, scholarships for soccer players are very limited. As I write this, the NCAA ceiling for men is the equivalent of 9.9 free rides, with women limited to 11. That's not a lot when you consider that most squads have at least double that number of players.

To stretch such limited resources, most schools will offer but a few full rides and divide the remainder into fractions. Unlike the American football coach, who has up to 85 scholarships at his disposal, the soccer coach can't afford to make mistakes. To sleep better at night, soccer coaches will dig deep into your background to discover if you're self-motivated. They want to know if you're continuing to work on your weaknesses or if you hit a plateau in the 10th grade and are content to play every ball with your stronger foot.

It's important that you make every effort to improve in all four categories listed above. To be sure, it's most difficult to make strides in the physical domain. I could have spent 20 hours a day working on sprinting techniques, and I would never have been a serious threat to Carl Lewis or, for that matter, to Cobi Jones, Eric Wynalda, or Ernie Stewart. But by putting in an appropriate amount of time, I was able to become slightly faster. And very often that extra half step is the difference in being able to successfully execute a tackle instead of being beaten.

Understand that college soccer is much more physically demanding than either scholastic or club ball. Professional soccer is much more physically demanding than the college game. And international soccer is far more physically demanding than all of them. But for now, let's stick with the college level. To be able to succeed in college, look to improve your speed, strength, and flexibility. Consult a qualified trainer to help develop a regimen that best suits your needs.

When you're about to go to college, you must get far more fit than you've ever been before. You have no idea just how taxing the game is until you're actually at that level. Whatever you assume to be a sufficient degree of fitness is probably inadequate.

Very few scholastic/club products are prepared to cope with the physical element of college ball. They really don't know how fit they

© Jon Van Woerden

Fig. 10.6.　Believe it or not, Cobi Jones came to college as a walk-on with great speed but limited skills. Through hard work and intelligence, he added enough skill and savvy to become a National Team player and an MLS star.

have to be to play at a higher level where the ball is in play more and people do a lot more off-the-ball running. Because the demands are much greater in games, the demands in training have to be proportionately greater as well.

Being anything less than fully fit makes it unlikely that you'll be able to show well in preseason. And then, during the season, you'll be in danger of overcompensating, which can lead to injury. The physical demands placed on you during those two-a-day or, in some cases, three-a-day preseason sessions are sure to test your psychological toughness, too.

© Wilfried Witters/hamburg

Fig. 10.7.   As in the change from high school to college, my transition to the pros demanded hard physical training to improve my athleticism and allow me to compete.

Unless you've traveled internationally with a club, state, regional, or national team, you're probably in for a shock. Even if you've had the benefit of such tours, you'll be in a different environment from the one you're living now. You'll be away from home and rooming with a stranger who probably comes from a background different from your own. After having been an important member or perhaps even the star of your club or scholastic team, you're now the proverbial low man (or woman) on the totem pole. There may even be times when it seems as if the coach who recruited you no longer remembers who you are.

You arrived on campus thinking that you'd not only make the varsity but that you'd be a starter. The next thing you know, you're left in the dark. It wasn't that long ago that you watched a Division I game and thought to yourself, "How come he didn't control that ball? It looked easy." But now you realize that the speed of play is such that what looked simple from the stands is perplexing on the pitch.

The practices are exhausting, and you have muscles aching in places you didn't even know you had muscles. To top it all off, soon you'll be taking classes that are more challenging than you've ever faced before. And you're on your own. You're homesick for your sweetheart, your family (yes, even your younger brother!), and your friends. You must now make decisions for yourself that your parents used to make for you, such as what to eat, when to get to bed, and how much to party. Poor choices will have major consequences. Your maturity—heck, your character—are being put to the test. And you'd be surprised at how many talented kids don't answer that call.

Don't be afraid to phone mom or dad or one of your previous coaches to get a morale boost. And it's okay to have some doubts—as long as you view them as challenges to be overcome and not as insurmountable obstacles. As an athlete, you should want to be tested. It's up to you to forget about the odds and the circumstances. Instead, focus on working hard in every moment of every practice to separate yourself from others who lack the mental toughness to advance themselves when the chips are down.

As the last few paragraphs illustrate, it's not always the most physically talented player who survives. Very often, it's the person with superior character. That's why college coaches want to know about your "total package" before they invite you into their program or offer you a scholarship. Your grades reflect to what degree your priorities are in order. The recommendations of your teachers will be studied with care. So will the way that you relate to others. Some coaches ask equipment room managers and custodians for their opinions of high school athletes. They want to know if you treat everyone with respect or if you're a jerk who shows off for your friends by belittling people you look down upon.

Having experienced four seasons of competition at UCLA, I have come to appreciate why attitude and behavior are germane to the recruiting process. Act as if you are always being observed, graded, analyzed, and compared to somebody else. A bad reputation limits your options. To play at the highest level that your ability allows requires a commitment to be the best that you can be in everything that you do. It's just that simple.

The ratio of available scholarships to worthy candidates remains distressingly disproportionate. The little things you do well are often the difference between receiving or not receiving aid or in determining how much aid you'll be awarded.

THOSE WHO GET AHEAD

Generally speaking, the players who make Division I rosters are more technically and athletically proficient than their lower-division counterparts. They tend to take the game more seriously. But generalizations don't always hold. There have been plenty of outstanding players at the Division II and III levels, including a handful who have gone on to our National Teams Program.

At the intercollegiate level, the player with mediocre technique with the best chance of becoming a decent role player is the great athlete. But a great athlete shouldn't be content with that. If you fall in this category, imagine how outstanding you could become by marrying your athleticism to great skill and tactical awareness. Regardless of your athletic base, don't ever be satisfied with the level you're at. Don't be content to be the best kid in your neighborhood, state, or region. Think big. Can you be the best in the United States? If you are the best in the United States, is that good enough to help our National Team win more international games, or are you just the best on a U.S. team that can't compete with an excellent foreign side? Take the attitude that no matter how good you are, you can *always* get better. This is true of every individual and of every team.

The bottom line at the college level is that coaches are looking for players who can legitimately play the game. Everyone defines "play the game" slightly differently, but what it comes down to is that they want athletes who can execute as a soccer player must. Either you can play the game already, or someone must see that you have the potential to play and contribute to the team within a year or two.

THERE IS NO OFF-SEASON

Before you know it, the soccer season is over. But to a real soccer player, the season never ends. Even we pros can improve our skills tremendously if we work hard enough. The best time to improve is during your developmental years. Don't be satisfied merely to put in more time than your teammates. The true standard is global. Put in as much time, or more, than the motivated Brazilian or Italian youngster who spends two to three hours daily engaged in some aspect of the game. If you aren't willing to pay the price, don't moan when you don't reap the rewards. If you want to be the best, you have

© Jon Van Woerden

Fig. 10.8. Michelle Akers' leg muscles testify to the hard work necessary to excel in soccer.

to spend the time. Only a few will make it, and fewer still will make it out of sheer athletic ability. It's your motivation and your desire that will carry you through.

To put things in perspective, our typical scholastic season lasts less than three months. The college season isn't much better. Preseason training begins in mid-August. The four teams that get to the last stages of the NCAA tournament finish their season in early December. That's not even four months. Even with a spring program, our best student-athletes formally compete less than half as long as the better players in Europe.

I feel safe in asserting that UCLA is as good as any school at preparing its better players for pro soccer. But even with the superb facilities, Sigi's

If you aren't willing to pay the price, don't moan when you don't reap the rewards.

great coaching, and a roster full of ambitious teammates, those kids are not living in as thorough a soccer environment as they would be had they joined a pro club as a teenager, as young players in Brazil and other countries do. Almost all of today's Bruin players spend many hours working on their skills during their free time. It was that level of commitment that got these athletes to UCLA in the first place, and it's that level which, they hope, will keep them moving ahead.

While hard work is rewarding, too much of a good thing isn't always advisable. There will be times when your body and brain need a break. You know your own requirements better than anyone else. Having had to push yourself through practices and games, there may be times when putting your ball in the closet for a week or two proves rejuvenating and more productive than working on your own.

OTHER FACTORS TO CONSIDER

I'm convinced that Diego Maradona couldn't have played at UCLA. Sounds crazy, yes? Being the best in the world when it comes to skill, tactical awareness, and athleticism will make any coach drool. But it doesn't guarantee that the admissions department will be impressed. Don't be fooled by incidents at some schools where academically deficient individuals are admitted because the height of their vertical jump negates the depths of their SAT scores. College soccer is big and is becoming bigger, but it's hard to imagine that in the foreseeable future it will become the kind of cash cow that football and basketball are. Consequently, don't expect strings to be pulled to get you into a school or program—you'll have to earn it on your own.

The best soccer schools tend to be very strong academically, and those guys you see kicking a ball are real students. To be sure, your athletic prowess may weigh in your favor if you're a borderline case. A school that requires a B+ average and 1100s (math and verbal combined) on your SATs may be willing to gamble if you have a B and a 1075 composite. But you darn sure won't get in if you aren't at least close to the standard.

As is true of being a versatile player, being a legitimate student-athlete greatly increases your options and can significantly enhance your financial picture. Countless student-athletes have qualified for handsome non-athletic scholarships because the soccer coach helped pave their way. This means that you could get a nice chunk of your costs defrayed, even at a Division III institution (which is prohibited from offering athletic scholarships) or at a school with limited athletic funds to disburse. Yes, hit the practice field hard. But always hit the books just as hard (if not harder).

Academic Eligibility in the NCAA

As of this writing, there are several standards you must meet before you step onto that soccer field for the college of your choice. If you wish to be eligible to compete as a freshman at the Division I or II level, you must be certified by the NCAA Initial-Eligibility Clearinghouse. This process begins with your obtaining a form and other materials. Ask your guidance counselor, or call the Clearinghouse at 319-337-1492 for details. In addition to having earned a high school diploma, you'll need successful completion of at least 13 "core" academic courses. Your high school principal determines which courses are in this category. Included among them must be at least two years each of a social science, math, and science, and either four (if you're headed for a Division I college) or three years of English (Division II). You must have maintained no less than a 2.0 grade-point average (on a 4.0-point scale) with a composite SAT score of 700 or better or scored 17 or more on your ACT test. However, there's a catch. The lower your GPA, the higher your SAT or ACT scores must be. As I write this, the sliding scale demands that a student with a 2.5 average needs only the minimum SAT or ACT score. But if your average is 2.0 you must have scored no less than 21 on your ACT or 900 on your SAT. NCAA standards are subject to constant modifications. Check with your guidance counselor for up-to-date information.

The Recruiting Process

Most folks assume that schools recruit athletes. This is only partly true. There are also a lot of cases in which a player recruits a school. NCAA regulations prohibit a Division I soccer coach from phoning you prior to July 1 after the completion of your junior year. They may not write to you until September 1 at the start of your junior year.

However, if *you* initiate contact by writing prior to those dates the coach is then allowed to respond.

Sigi told me that he's favorably impressed when a prospect sends a personal letter that's well-written and neat. This is but one example of how the enlightened scholastic athlete can obtain an edge. But you must also be alert not to violate any of the many NCAA rules, some of which are incredibly petty. To show you just how stringent some regulations are, the NCAA's 1995-96 Guide for the College-Bound Student-Athlete lists under what circumstances you're allowed to engage in a contact with a college coach. A "contact" is defined as any discussion between the two of you in which you say "more than 'hello.'" So, if you're walking across a field after watching an intercollegiate match, don't tell the winning coach "nice game" or technically you'll be violating the rules!

You can also become a professional in the NCAA's eyes by entering into any agreement with an agent (even if it's for future representation), being paid for playing in an athletic contest (don't accept prize money from a Tuesday night bowling league!), or by playing on a team with pros. If you're ever in doubt, be sure to ask questions of the appropriate authorities before taking any action that could jeopardize your eligibility.

Despite some of the examples I just mentioned, the vast majority of NCAA restrictions make sense and were instituted for your protection. I do recommend that you call the NCAA to get a copy of that student-athlete guide, as it's filled with helpful advice. NCAA headquarters is located at 6201 College Boulevard, Overland Park, Kansas 66211-2422. Their phone number is 913-339-1906.

BUT PAUL, YOU STILL HAVEN'T ANSWERED MY QUESTION!

Yes, I know that I still haven't said where you should go and how you can get there. Even though I've headed a lot of overinflated balls on cold days, my memory isn't that bad!

• The greatest part of the equation involves a fit between your academic needs and what a school has to offer. You must also look at all other issues important to you, ranging from the ratio of faculty to students, size and location of the town, and what majors are offered. Your guidance counselor should be able to help you find a good fit. If one counselor isn't able to help you much, try another one. It's an occupation with a huge range of competency levels.

I chose UCLA because it was the best school for Paul Caligiuri among those institutions for whom I wanted to play soccer. The athletic program and the academic environment suited me well. I was fortunate. As someone with Youth National Team experience, I had a sufficiently high profile that they recruited me. But there is nothing to preclude you from taking the first step. If you're not recruited by the schools you're interested in, by all means initiate the first contact yourself.

• Once you've identified a few schools that you feel are right for you, write to the coach as early as possible. Your letter should be specific, giving reasons why you wish to attend that school and play

Fig. 10.9.   Mike Lapper (left) is one of several USA stars who attended UCLA.

in that program. Don't send what reads like a form letter in which you've just filled in the blanks. For example, if you want to play at Virginia, don't say, "I want to play for Virginia because you have a fine program." Instead, refer specifically to what you like about a program ("I enjoy watching and would enjoy playing the free-flowing style that your team uses, and I love the atmosphere of your home games at Klockner Stadium").

• Your words will help, but don't forget that a picture is worth a thousand words. After a coach (or one of the assistants) has responded and shown some interest in you, send a videotape of yourself in action. If possible, this tape should be fully prepared before you start your senior year. Make sure that the quality (both of the tape and your play) is sufficient to help your cause.

If your school tapes games, see if you can get together with someone from the audiovisual or athletic department to look through them. Not every school has the budget and/or inclination to tape games. If they don't, it's up to you to take initiative. Find someone with strong shoulders to volunteer. The vantage point should be from an elevated position, and the viewer shouldn't feel seasick after watching it. In most cases, a highlight film of your best moments is the way to go. Log game tapes by noting the counter number of highlights that involved you. Edit them into one presentation. You'd be amazed at how many tapes coaches receive where the "subject" touches the ball only 10 times in over an hour and the numbers on the uniforms make it impossible to know who the players are.

Don Rawson, who watched more than a few Titanic-like taping efforts while an assistant at Indiana University, told me that "many tapes actually destroy a kid's chances. Maybe his dad focused on him, but he wasn't moving off of the ball. We had kids send tapes when they weren't the best player on the field. We've said, 'The heck with number 10, let's get that number 8!' If I were sending a tape, I'd send one that really, truly highlights my ability. If you're a goal-scorer, send a tape of your goals and the positive near-misses, not the near-misses that were chokes. Only send a game tape if it's against a really tough opponent and you were really all over that game."

• Seeing is believing. Send a coach all of your schedules (school, club, state, regional, and/or ODP) well in advance. The coach will be impressed by your initiative, at least, even if he or she doesn't send a representative to take a look at you.

- As with applying for a job, a good reference can be of great help. Ask a well-respected player or coach who knows your game to get in touch with the coach of the school you're interested in or to write a letter promoting your cause.

REALISTIC EXPECTATIONS

Arrive on campus (a few weeks ahead of the rest of the incoming freshman class) with realistic expectations. Any coach who promises an incoming candidate a starting position is either making a big mistake or just isn't being forthright. You should only expect the chance to win a job if an opening is available. The athlete in you is entitled to an opportunity to train and improve. Never expect or demand that you will automatically be a starter or will play in a certain position. Neither you nor your coach can know who will walk on to the team or if you'll wilt under the pressure of college ball.

Expect to go to a school where you are a student first and foremost. Ultimately, it's how well you fare in the classroom that will have the greatest influence on your future.

COLLEGE, THE PROS, AND YOU

You may be well aware that Jovan Kirovski left the comforts of his southern California home at 16 to become an apprentice professional at Manchester United. Given Jovan's incredible talent and tremendous passion to excel at soccer, that decision made sense for him. But what you may not know is that he had the foresight to continue his education in England. Jovan worked out an arrangement with United whereby he would have his afternoons free to allow him to earn his high school diploma. As I write this, he is progressing toward a college degree.

During the heyday of the old NASL, a handful of Americans went straight from high school to the pros. If you're so fortunate to receive such an offer, carefully weigh the pros and cons of both avenues. Should you decide to turn pro, consider securing the services of a reputable agent who can negotiate on your behalf. Among your top priorities should be to have that team guarantee (through a bond) that it will set aside enough money to pay for your college education.

More likely that not, you'll attempt to play college ball. There will be many huge decisions that you will be called upon to make in your life. Of these, selecting which college to attend is usually the first of the major ones. Try, if possible, to visit campuses during the soccer season. Seek out the players, and don't be shy about asking them direct questions about the coach and staff. They can fill you in better than anyone about important matters such as the balance between athletics and academics. Find out if they have a well thought-out tutorial program to assist student-athletes.

At UCLA, for example, Sigi carefully regulates the academics of all his players. He knows just how important your schoolwork is, both to your future and your athletic performance. He understands that the athlete who feels burdened about falling behind on his studies is unlikely to fully concentrate during practices and games. I know that can happen, because it happened to me. I can still vividly remember feeling so mentally drained and physically exhausted that I had to force myself to leave my room to study. The key to escaping from that funk was learning how to manage my time more efficiently. I was told by an academic advisor to literally draw up a daily planner a week in advance. I consulted it to know when I would eat, study, practice, and sleep. Such a planning schedule helps you make the best use of your time and also gives you peace of mind—you don't have to worry about how you'll find the time to get something done, because it's already on the schedule.

Expect to miss some classes and some tests while your college team is traveling. Playing catch-up is tough stuff, especially with the added time demands of participating in intercollegiate athletics. Thus, it's best to get ahead of your studies during any of the rare lull periods.

Don't rush when deciding which university to pick. I recommend backing off if a school puts you under pressure for an early answer. So, too, with negative recruiting. An institution that offers a first rate soccer program and a healthy academic environment will entice you based on its own merits. There should be no need to criticize another school.

But this advice assumes that you have options. That will only be the case if you make an honest attempt to improve all four key aspects of your game and are both a good student and a solid citizen. The more choices you're able to create for yourself, the better the odds will be that you'll have a great experience in college. The bottom line is that your attitude, work ethic, and preparation are what will most determine your future. I find it exciting to think that some of you reading this book will go on to become better players and better students than I was.

Every recent generation of American players has improved upon its immediate predecessor. The first wave of natives in the old NASL proved that Americans could be role players at a top club level. By the middle of the 1980s we were good enough to become one of the more prominent national teams in FIFA's CONCACAF Region (which consists of North and Central American and Caribbean nations).

Less than a decade later, we had several of our top players doing well in the best European leagues, and our National Team managed victories over England, Ireland, and, of course, those shockers over Colombia in the 1994 World Cup and Argentina in the 1995 Copa America.

Fig. 10.10. My teammates and I have enjoyed many glorious moments, like celebrating Eric's great free-kick goal against the Swiss in the 1994 World Cup. It's my dream that one of you reading this book will help our National Team reach even greater heights.

Our Women's program has been good and is getting better. The 1991 World Championship proved that the USA is a leader in that category. With Mia Hamm, Michelle Akers, Carin (Jennings) Gabarra, and Julie Foudy, we have produced some of the top female players in the game, which was confirmed by our women's team taking the gold in the 1996 summer Olympics.

Now it's time for one of our men to become that first bona fide superstar mentioned in the same breath as the best players in the sport. I really hope that when that player emerges, his background includes steps he took from having read this book. Nothing would give me greater pleasure than to live long enough to witness the day when American athletes lift the World Cup over their heads.

I hope that you've found the time spent reading this book worthwhile and that it helps you reach your potential. Think of this book as but one piece of a giant puzzle that includes watching pro games, asking questions, viewing tapes, and, above all, playing as often as possible out of the sheer love of the sport. Good luck, and keep on kickin'!

Index

About the Authors

Paul Caligiuri, one of the greatest players in U.S. soccer history, is one of only two U.S. players to have earned more than 100 caps. He is also one of the first American players to succeed overseas in the European soccer leagues. In 1986, Paul was the only American picked to play in the FIFA World All-Star Game, and he was named the USA's Player of the Year. In 1988, he earned a spot on the U.S. Olympic Soccer team and started in all three U.S. Games played in Seoul, South Korea. The following year, Paul

played a pivotal role in the U.S. team's historic World Cup qualifying-round game against Trinidad and Tobago. His magnificent 30-yard, left-footed volley produced the only goal of the game and gave the United States its first berth in a World Cup since 1950.

Paul has been a vital performer for the U.S. National Soccer Team since making his debut in 1984. He was a member of the 1990 and 1994 U.S. World Cup teams, a defender on the USA squads that won the U.S. Cup '92 and U.S. Cup '95, and an all-star on the U.S. team that reached the semifinal round of the 1995 Copa America. In addition, Paul was a member of the 1985 UCLA soccer team, which won the NCAA Division I championship game.

Paul is a member of the Columbus Crew. When he isn't playing soccer, he enjoys golfing, participating in water sports, and attending youth soccer activities.

Dan Herbst is a freelance writer whose work has appeared in *Sports Illustrated* and *Sport Magazine*, as well as in such soccer publications as *Soccer Junior*, the *1994 World Cup Game Program*, and *'94 World Cup Daily*. He has written seven books and has covered soccer as a professional writer since the 1970s. Dan is also a former college soccer player and a nationally licensed coach. In his free time he enjoys watching and coaching soccer, bowling, and golf.

© Steve Slade

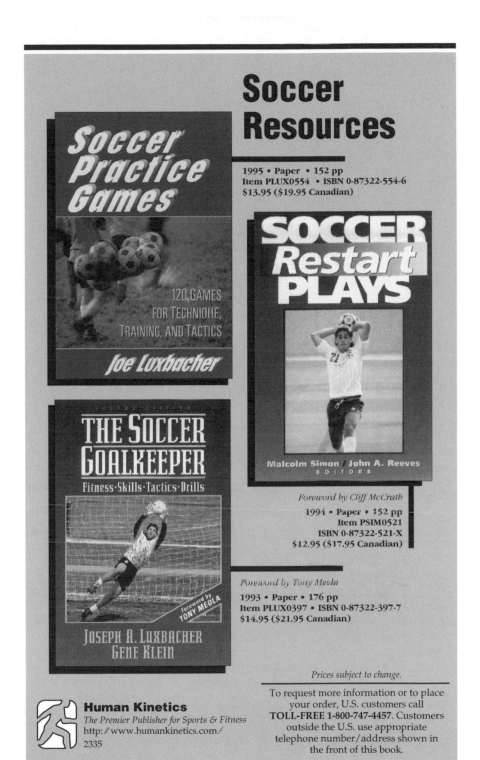